SCIENCE & HUMANISM

Towards A Unified World View

Ye Ca Buddha atita ca,

Ye ca Buddha anagatha,

paccipannah ca ye Buddha,

aham vandami sabbada

(Dhajagga Sutta, Samyutta Nikaya)
XI (I) (3)

'To the Enlightened ones of the past,

And to the Enlightened ones yet to come,

To the Enlightened ones of present as well,

Always do I pay my obeisance'.

SCIENCE & HUMANISM

Towards A Unified World View

Ye Ca Buddha atita ca,

Ye ca Buddha anagatha,

paccipannah ca ye Buddha,

aham vandami sabbada

(Dhajagga Sutta, Samyutta Nikaya)
XI (I) (3)

'To the Enlightened ones of the past,

And to the Enlightened ones yet to come,

To the Enlightened ones of present as well,

Always do I pay my obeisance'.

SCIENCE & HUMANISM
Towards A Unified World View

Ye Ca Buddha atita ca,

Ye ca Buddha anagatha,

paccipannah ca ye Buddha,

aham vandami sabbada

(Dhajagga Sutta, Samyutta Nikaya)
XI (I) (3)

'To the Enlightened ones of the past,

And to the Enlightened ones yet to come,

To the Enlightened ones of present as well,

Always do I pay my obeisance'.

FOREWORD

It is a real pleasure for me to write a few words about this book on Science and Humanism by Professors P.L. Dhar and R.R. Gaur of Indian Institute of Technology, Delhi.

Today, the world is facing a challenge which, in a fundamental sense, affects its very survival. There is the horror of nuclear weapons and other powerful instruments of mass destruction; there is the rapid degradation of our environment and depletion of resources; there is the astonishingly rapid expansion in the use of drugs and the infection of AIDS and there is the new phenomenon of organized militancy.

There was never in man's history more knowledge, especially science and technology, than available today, and yet, never before in human history was there greater tyranny, social injustice, distrust and rampant violence affecting almost every aspect of human life and relationships. A dismal and agonising situation such as the present one gives to this book a value and relevance and significance which cannot be over-emphasized. We need to create a mass awareness of the crucial danger facing mankind today. The foundation for this awareness has to be necessarily in our educational institutions beginning with the schools. But the institutions of higher learning, particularly in Science and Technology have an important responsibility of orienting their teaching and research in consonance with the new challenges facing the modern world.

I feel, the present book should be a must-reading for our science and engineering students.

There is so much knowledge and yet so much violence because, we have failed to give serious attention in our education to the theme of 'human values' and how these can be practised in our lives. We have been trying to pursue science, ignoring the linkage of Science with Humanism. We need to emphasize and cultivate the fusion of science with morality to their mutual benefit. In the profound and inspiring words of Einstein:

> The most important human endeavour is the striving for morality in our actions. Only morality in our actions can provide the inner balance and this is vital for our very existence. To bring this to clear consciousness and make it a living force is perhaps the foremost task of education.

Towards this goal so eloquently emphasized by Einstein, the present book makes a significant contribution. For this, I should again like to congratulate the authors and wish them success.

Prof. D.S. KOTHARI

PREFACE

Science and Humanism are two complementary aspects of human endeavour towards fulfilment of the ultimate aspirations of human life, viz., peace and happiness. While science equips us with the knowledge of external nature and technology, utilising this storehouse of knowledge, provides the 'means' to achieve certain 'ends', the 'ends' themselves must be determined using the wisdom of Humanism. Such an integration of 'knowledge' with 'wisdom' is crucial to the success of all our endeavours. Any tendency towards violation of this complementarity by neglect of one aspect in favour of the other is bound to be catastrophic.

The crisis of modern civilization which is so much advanced in science and technology and yet appears to be on the brink of a precipice can be understood in the light of the above cardinal truth. As Bertrand Russell succinctly put it,

> "We are in the middle of a race between human skill as to means and human folly as to ends—unless men increase in wisdom as much as in knowledge, increase of knowledge will be increase of sorrow"

To clearly appreciate the nature of interaction and complementarity between Science and Humanism (and its impact on technology and society) and to work towards their proper integration is the most urgent need of mankind today. The book addresses itself to this vital issue.

In the first part, it presents an in-depth analysis of the crisis of modern civilization in the light of the above perspective.

It begins with highlighting modern predicament which may be summarised as follows:

> If we discard the present model of development, how else do we live? and if we continue to embrace it, shall we at all live?

Modern technology which is the prime instrument of our progress is then critically evaluated. It is shown that features like reductionism, centralisation and mass production etc. which have been the cause of rapid 'success' of modern technology are also responsible for its multiple maladies. Thus, it is concluded that the global maladies such as environmental degradation, resource depletion etc. are not just the result of 'misuse' of technology but that the inherent nature of modern technology is anti-ecological and unsustainable.

Modern technology has been born and nurtured in the materialistic worldview which has correspondingly shaped its characteristic features. How such a worldview developed during past few centuries is traced historically in Chapter 3. Factors like the growth of the mechanistic-reductionistic philosophies, the decay of religion, science-religion dichotomy and the revival of materialism are discussed at length.

In Chapter 4, the correlation between various aspects of modern predicament and the materialistic paradigm, e.g., materialism and social strife, materialism and ecology, materialism and dehumanisation etc. is discussed. It emerges from this analysis that the prevailing materialistic paradigm is the root cause of various technological maladies of our times. This part of the book ends on a hopeful note indicating positive signs of the emergence of an alternative, non-materialistic, holistic world view which if properly understood and implemented can provide a way to get out of the present predicament.

The second part of the book discusses from various angles, the notion and implications of the holistic worldview. To begin with, Chapter 5 briefly illustrates that the philosophical implications of 20th century science (as elaborated by Capra, Sheldrake, Pribram, Bohm, Prigogine and others) point towards a non-mechanistic, interconnected nature of reality which is quite similar to the view points of eastern mystics. In the newly-emerging understanding both Science and Humanism project the same unified worldview.

Chapter 6 describes the second significant factor contributing to the emergence of the new worldview, viz., the 'renaissance' of eastern wisdom which originated from India towards the end of the nineteenth century. Beginning with Swami Vivekananda, a number of modern saints such as Swami Ram Tirth, Sri Aurbindo etc. scientifically re-expounded in the idiom of our times, the essence of ancient humanistic philosophies. Mahatma Gandhi practically demonstrated the strength and efficacy of the holistic paradigm in the modern context.

This chapter also brings out the fallacy of the sensory (materialistic) enjoyment and its misery-mounting mechanism. It, further, asserts that self-purification or self-realization is the only true path to abiding peace and happiness, and forms the bedrock of humanism as well.

Chapter 7 gives a brief review of the various methods of self- realization, the practical approaches to the arduous task of moving out of the illusion of one's identification with body and mind and moving towards one's identication with the whole reality.

Finally, the last chapter presents a glimpse of the alternative, holistic vision of development. Which shall be sustainable as well as commensurate with the purpose of life. To work towards fulfilling such a vision is the real challenge that we face so that humanity may live on peacefully and happily.

This book has been written with two objectives in mind. Firstly, the authors feel very strongly that the issues involved must be introduced to all science and engineering students at the college level. We had started such a course at I.I.T. Delhi in 1983 and have taught it almost every semester since then. The overwhelming response of the students has, in fact, been the main motivation for the authors to consolidate the lecture notes evolved over last eight years to serve as a text book.

The second purpose of the book is to motivate the general reader (with a little familiarity with modern science) to think in this direction. If the book can induce some of its readers to appreciate the root cause of the maladies of modern times and to begin transformation in tune with the holistic world-view, the authors would consider their efforts fruitful.

We would like to express our deep sense of gratitude to Prof. D.S. Kothari, the octogenarian philospher-scientist and educationist of great eminence who was instrumental not only in getting this course initiated at IIT Delhi, but also in motivating us (and many others) to work in this area. We are especially indebted to him for writing the foreword to this book.

Our friend, Shri T.S. Ananthu, who had been fully devoted to research in this area at Gandhi Peace Foundation for more than a decade and is presently experimenting with implementation of the new world view at 'Navdarshnam', Bangalore, has helped us in many ways to understand this subject and to develop the course. We are very thankful to Shri Ananthu and his wife Jyothi, for their help and encouragement.

We would also like to express our sincere gratitude to Swami Sanatan Shri (of Lucknow) and Swami Bhoomanad Tirtha (of Trichur) for the inspiration we received through personal interactions with them. To our Vipassana mediation teacher, Shri S.N. Goenka, we shall remain grateful for showing us the practical way to self-purification.

Many colleagues, and students at I.I.T. have also encouraged us to complete this work and made valuable suggestions for improving the quality of the course and thereby of this book. We would like to especially mention, Prof. (Mrs.) P. Mathur, Dr. S.D. Sharma, Prof. M.S. Sodha, Dr. Y.S. Satya, Dr. Sunil Kale and Mr. Aromar Revi.

Lastly, but not the least, we would like to express our thanks to the members of our family, especially our wives Susheela Dhar and Santosh Gaur, for bearing with long periods of absence directly or indirectly related to our preoccupation with the work related to this book.

P.L. Dhar
R.R. Gaur

CONTENTS

PART I

MODERN PREDICAMENT

1 WE ARE PROGRESSING

"...it was the age of wisdom, it was the age of foolishness; it was the epoch of belief, it was the epoch of incredulity; it was the season of light, it was the season of darkness; it was the spring of hope, it was the winter of despair; we had everything before us, we had nothing before us...."

–Charles Dickens,
Tale of Two Cities (1859)

As the fateful twentieth century is hurtling speedily towards its close, it seems worthwhile to take stock of its achievements and failures. Most certainly this century has been an epoch of phenomenal change. In fact, this period may be visualized as the Great Median strip running down the centre of human history. 'The world of today', asserts Kenneth Boulding '... is as different from the world in which I was born as that world was from Julius Caesar's. I was born in the middle of human history, to date roughly. Almost as much has happened since I was born as happened before'.

Countless and awe-inspiring are our achievements: Atom has been smashed and the gene decoded; the space has been conquered and we have ushered in green revolution, promising an era of abundance free from hunger and poverty. We can communicate instantaneously with persons anywhere on the globe and can travel faster than sound. And we have the micro-chip which promises to surpass the best of human brains.

Penicillin and hundreds of other such wonder-drugs are now with us to provide rapid relief from gruesome pains and hitherto incurable diseases. Sophisticated methods of diagnostics are available to scan almost every interior tissue of the human body. Surgery has advanced to a level that any vital part of the body can be replaced.

Vagaries of weather need not torment us anymore as we are able to provide comfort-conditioning not only in our dwellings and places of work but even in the vehicles.

The list of miraculous achievements of modern age could go on almost endlessly. Such is the success story of the grand progress march of the twentieth century man. And all this has been possible with the power of modern science and technology, or to be more precise, western science and technology. The industrial revolution which sprouted in Europe three centuries ago, has come in full bloom in this century and today holds the entire globe in its spell. The western nations which pioneered this development have rightfully acquired the status of 'developed' nations and all the rest in the world, irrespective of their culture, ideologies and political systems have unanimously accepted them as their ideals. Consequently the world today is fully geared to actualize this model of development as expeditiously as possible.

However, with the widespread adoption of this model of development, an epilogue to this Book of Laurels of our age is emerging which sounds some discordant notes in the symphony of achievements. Gradually, it is becoming evident that the modern industrialized development is not without tears. The table given below provides a brief outline of the unpleasant aspects of modern 'progress'. Prepared by the Stanford Research Institute's Centre[2] for the Study of Social Policy, this table lists selected successes and associated maladies of the present technological era.

Table 1: Benefits and Detriments of Modern Development

	Benefits of 'Success'	Detriments of 'Success'
1.	Reduced Infant and Adult Mortality rates	Regional overpopulation; problems of the aged.
2.	Highly developed Science and Technology	Hazards of mass destruction through nuclear and biological weapons; vulnerability of specialization, threats to privacy and freedom (e.g. surveillance technology, bio – engineering).
3.	Machine Replacement of manual and routine labour	Exacerbated unemployment.
4.	Advances in communication and transportation	Increasing air, noise and land pollution; 'information overload', vulnerability of a complex society to breakdown; disruption of human biological rhythms.
5.	Efficient production systems	Dehumanization of ordinary work.
6.	Affluence; material growth	Increased per capita consumption of energy and goods, leading to pollution and depletion of earth's resources.
7.	Satisfaction of basic needs	Worldwide revolutions of 'rising expectations', rebellion against non-meaningful work.
8.	Expanded power of human choice	Unanticipated consequences of technological applications; management breakdown as regards control of these.
9.	Expanded wealth of developed nations; pockets of affluence	Increasing gap between 'have' and 'have-not' nations, frustration of the revolutions of rising expectations; exploitation; pockets of poverty.

What is really alarming is the fact that as more and more people are embracing this pattern of development, the maladies engendered by this transformation are blowing up into multiple, global crises of unprecedented nature which threaten not only the peace, health and happiness but even the very survival of humanity.

In recent years, a large number of people, intellectuals as well as ordinary men and women, throughout the world, have become conscious of the enormous dangers of modern development. A vast body of popular literature has appeared[4-7] in last two decades, highlighting this dark side of our 'progress'. The Club of Rome, which is a worldwide body of concerned intellectuals and distinguished professionals, has brought out a series of very revealing reports on this 'Predicament of Mankind'. In the foreword to one of these reports[3], Aurelio Peccei and Alexander King describe the modern predicament as follows:

Modern man, despite the wonderful body of knowledge and information that he has accumulated and the means to apply it, appears to be muddling ahead as if he were blind or drugged, staggering from one crisis to another. It is increasingly evident that he is unsure where he is going or where he wants to go beyond the next few tentative steps, yet he has received all sorts of signals that he is treading fields that are heavily mined and require thorough exploration and mapping,...the inquiry into what we are up to, what we can or should do with ourselves and future generations, should undoubtedly come first, if for no other reason than because without an overall design our frenzied activities can but give rise to colossal disorder – which is precisely what is beginning to occur today.

Unfortunately, the society today is so inebriated with the 'benefits' of 'progress' that it seems to be in no mood to slow down the pace of its frenzied activities and inquire into "what are we up to?" The people attempting to point out the seriousness of the problems facing mankind are often dubbed as 'doomsday prophets' and conveniently ignored. Such is the faith of society on modern science and technology that it is implicitly assumed – even in teeth of glaring evidence – that solutions will be found to all these problems in the near future. Thus nuclear energy was (and in many nations, including India, continues to be) seen as the solution to rapid depletion of fossil fuels which are the chief propellants of modern civilization. The Chernobyl accident, the revelations that almost all nuclear reactors are silently waging a 'chemical warfare' on the inhabitants of the surrounding areas, and the frightening possibilities of what could happen with thousands of tons of highly radioactive "wastes"* scattered inside the earth all over the globe are certainly weaning away nations from the nuclear option but the faith, that an alternative would be found (fusion energy, we are told is free from hazards) still persists. The result: we never ask the Tolstoyian question, "How much energy does a man need?"

Almost similar arguments are advanced by protagonists of modern technology to alleviate the fears of society with regard to other serious maladies like ecological imbalances, depletion of metals and minerals, increasing violence and crime, etc. Better pollution control gadgets, we are assured, would remove environmental pollution; plastics will replace metals, and if need be, we could mine neighbouring planets; and better equipped police force would mitigate violence and crime.

It, therefore, seems imperative to undertake an indepth study of modern technology, to understand its fundamental characteristics and then make a dispassionate appraisal of its capabilities. In Chapter 2 we address ourselves to this task.

---

* which would remain radio- active for thousands of years!

NOTES

(1) Alvin Toeffler : *Future Shock*, Pan Books Ltd., pp. 22. This, now classic, book gives a highly readable account of the problems arising from rapid changes in the society.

(2) Houston, Jean : "Prometheus Rebound: An Inquiry into Technological Growth and Psychological Change", Chapter 14 in *Alternatives to Growth* edited by Donella Meadows, p. 277.

(3) Laszlo, E : "Goals for Mankind" - 5th Report of the Club of Rome series on *The Predicament of Mankind*, (Foreword, pp. vii).

(4) All the Reports of Club of Rome on *The Predicament of Mankind*.

(5) Schumacher, E.F. : *Small is Beautiful*, ABACUS, London, 1974.

(6) Capra, Fritjof :, *The Turning Point*, Flamingo, 1983. A sequel to Capra's bestseller, the *Tao of Physics*, wherein he brings out in detail how our clinging to the mechanistic worldview is responsible for bringing us perilously close to destruction; and how a new holistic vision consistent with the findings of modern physics and other important areas of modern science could become the" turning point" in all aspects of our culture.

(7) Huxley, A., *The Human Situation*, Triad Granada, 1978.

2 MODERN TECHNOLOGY AS AN INSTRUMENT OF PROGRESS

If it's just the noise of progress that is beating in our ears

we could look beyond the turbulence and soothe our gnawing fears

Man is drowning in his own success, and hapless is his hope

If our science and technology is but a rotten rope.

...Kenneth E. Boulding
A Ballad of Ecological Awareness

Modern technology is usually hailed as the great benefactor of mankind which promises to usher an era of abundance and thus alleviate all human misery and sufferings. It is seen as the prime factor responsible for relieving the material wants of a sizable section of mankind and the only way to achieve the same for the starving millions of the 'third world'. Technology is viewed as a great liberating force, "slavery became immoral when it became technically obsolete" says Gerard Piel[1] and even social democracy is only a by-product of technology[2].

While many of these assertions of the advocates of modern technology are open to serious criticism, even without doing so, it can be easily seen that modern technology is not the proper instrument for 'progress'. The large number of serious maladies which besiege our modern civilisation are in fact the consequences of this very technology and cannot be wished away as leisure-time blabberings of its 'ungrateful' beneficiaries. While some of the maladies enumerated in the previous chapter can be directly related to technology—environmental pollution and nuclear-armament, for example—others like growing inequity, increasing tension and violence, etc. seem to be of too abstract a nature to be affected by technology. Thus, the protagonists of the technological culture would often dismiss the later category of maladies as social maladies 'not related to technology' and would attempt to project the former as aberrations, or at best, errors of judgement or omission which could be easily taken care of by more 'advanced technology'. Thus, they would recommend intensification of R&D effort on better pollution control gadgets to reduce environmental pollution, more sophisticated mineral extraction techniques to ward off resource depletion and improved shelters to survive nuclear fallouts.

A careful analysis, however, reveals that this is not the case. The way modern technology has developed—and continues to develop—it has acquired, and is further strengthening certain characteristics which, in the long run, are bound to give rise to the type of problems which are surfacing now. Very radical changes in the basic objectives of technology are necessary if we wish to avoid these serious shortcomings of modern technology.

Technology and Human Welfare

It is generally accepted that technology is the tool which enables application of science for human welfare, — a sort of bridge between science and humanism. It, therefore, follows that the 'character' of technology will bear a strong imprint of what is understood by the term 'human-welfare'. Now, if we were to find out an answer to this question from the current protagonists of modern technology—whether it be the managing director of a big multinational corporation or a small industrialist in a poor 'third-world' country—it will undoubtedly emerge that for them human-welfare is synonymous with material well-being. All the modern technological innovations have their root in this concept of promotion of human welfare through creation of an abundance of goods and services within easy reach of all. Of course, whether these goods and services really reach the 'needy masses', and whether their provision is in consonance with their long-term 'good' does not seem to be the concern of anybody.

A look back into the past also reveals a similar picture. The genesis of modern technology can be traced back to eighteenth century, when the industrial revolution took place in the west. The outlook of the protagonists of technology at that time was, if anything, even more materialistic. The technology was for them a ginnie for making money as is corroborated by the horror tales of workers' plight in the mills in England. The transition to the era of modern technology as outlined in the sober words of Mumford brings it out amply:

> "There was a sharp shift in interest from life values to pecuniary values: the system of interests which only had been latent and which had been restricted in a great measure to the merchant and leisure classes now pervaded every walk of life. It was no longer sufficient for industry to provide a livelihood: it must create an independent fortune".

It was this crass materialistic attitude which saw workers only as 'tools' to an end and permitted and promoted their unremitting exploitation – a legacy which has been faithfully carried on, albeit under a more 'decent' garb of incentives and allowances, even in modern times.

It would thus be no exaggeration to say that modern technology has been born and brought up under a materialistic worldview and continues to be nourished by the same. In turn, this technology has become a powerful instrument for perpetuation of this worldview.

Materialistic worldview implies a belief that happiness lies solely in material acquisition. Thus it directly fosters consumerism and creates more and more demand for goods and services which can only be fulfilled by more technology. Of course, more technology also means improved advertising which strengthens the materialistic worldview and fuels the demand further. It is this consumerist culture which is at the

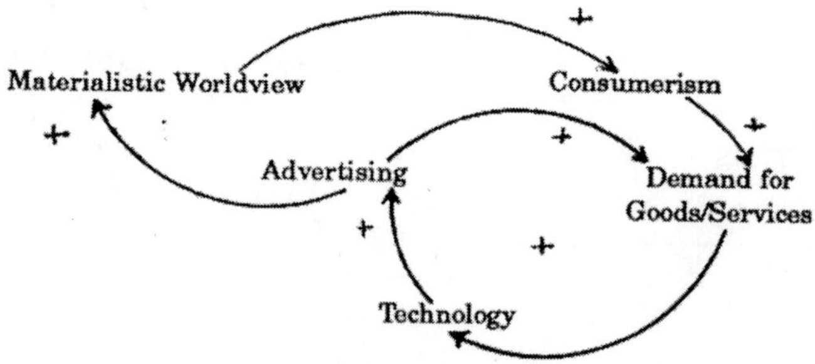

Fig. 1*

root of many of the maladies gripping our society. Exponential growth of industrial activity (needed to provide for exponentially growing demand) is bound to cause increasing pollution, howsoever good be the pollution control devices. And of course, at the societal level, increasing dependence on factory-made goods for daily living renders the social structure extremely fragile and vulnerable. Imagine the plight of a modern metropolis when, say, electricity fails for a few hours, or there is a breakdown in the main bread factory or in the milk chilling plant!

When materialism is the main propelling force behind technology, it is quite natural that out of various possible alternative technologies to satisfy a given need, the one guaranteeing maximum 'turnover' on investment would be adopted. In fact, the value system acts like a sieve to filter and phase out the 'undesirable' technologies from the 'desirable ones'. Consequently, through a process quite akin to that of natural selection, the strain of modern technology which has thus evolved over last two centuries is, in the words of Barry Commoner[6], "admirably suited to the economic needs of manufacturers", but poorly suited to the needs of the users. Thus, it does make economic sense to throw away toxic effluents into rivers and poisonous gases into atmosphere,

---

*In this diagram an arrow indicates that the variable at the tail of the arrow influences that at its head. A +ve sign implies that as the value of variable at the tail increases, so does the variable indicated at the head of the arrow

since any attempt at their treatment would only eat into the 'turnover'; and the obvious result of this ethic is Environmental Pollution.

The evolution of modern technology has thus naturally endowed it with numerous characteristics which are chiefly responsible for its phenomenal 'success'. A careful analysis reveals that these very characteristics—which could be termed as its genetic code—are also responsible for numerous technogenic maladies of modern age, thus calling into serious question the capability of modern technology as an instrument of 'progress'. Let us study some of these important distinguishing traits of modern technology.

Technology and Reductionism

Modern technology is by its very nature reductionistic, i.e., it demands the fragmentation of any task into smaller and simpler 'component-tasks' which could then be easily tackled by respective specialists. As has been succinctly brought out by Galbraith[4], "thus, and only thus, can organised knowledge be brought to bear on performance. Specifically, there is no way that organised knowledge can be brought to bear on the production of an automobile as a whole or even on the manufacture of a body or chassis. It can only be applied if the task is so subdivided that it begins to be coterminous with some established area of scientific or engineering knowledge. Though metallurgical knowledge cannot be applied to the manufacture of the whole vehicle, it can be used in the design of the cooling system of the engine block. While knowledge of mechanical engineering cannot be brought to bear on the manufacture of the vehicle, it can be applied to the machining of the crankshaft. While chemistry cannot be applied to the composition of the car as a whole, it can be used to decide on the composition of the finish or trim...."

This seems to be an accurate and a pretty innocuous description of modern technology so long as we do not realise the consequences of this attitude of reductionism inherent in modern technology. The modern mass-produced automobile is certainly a technological triumph, but only up to a point, the dividing line between success and failure being the factory door. So long as the automobile is being constructed, reductionist technology is admirably successful. However, once the automobile is allowed out of the factory and into the environment, it is a shocking failure. It becomes the agent which has rendered urban air carcinogenic, and burdened human bodies with nearly toxic levels of carbon monoxide and lead[6]. And what is true of an automobile seems to be valid for modern technology as a whole since reductionism is, by definition, anti-holistic[5], and therefore anti-ecological. Reductionism necessitates focussing attention on immediate consequences and thus promotes neglect of long-term consequences. As highlighted by Barry Commoner[6] through numerous examples, this reductionistic bias of modern technology is at the root of the ecological backlash surfacing now since it leads us to act massively on nature before we can be reasonably aware of the consequences.

Thus consider the consequences of introduction of chemical control of agricultural pests. A new synthetic chemical is designed to kill insects; its value is determined by testing the substance against this singular target. But this target—the insect pest—is in nature, an interconnected part of an elaborate whole, the ecosystem; and the new synthetic chemical not only kills some pests but also destroys the natural predators which normally regulate the pest population. The result : "With awesome regularity major outbreaks of insect pests have been induced by the use of modern contact killing insecticides—by stimulating the development of resistant strains and destroying the natural predators which ordinarily regulate the densities of pest population.[6]"

The reductionistic attitude is also the hallmark of modern medicine, which also falls within the purview of our definition of 'technology'. With its narrow specialisations, modern medicine now interprets every disease as an organ-specific disturbance caused most probably by attack of bacteria and/or viruses which are always on the prowl looking for unwary victims. The result: while we take 'medicines' to destroy these bacteria attacking a particular part of the body, these medicines themselves have 'side-effects' (often more serious than the original disease) on other parts of the body.

Or consider the consequences of reductionistic bias of modern technology when applied to construct a hydroelectric power station. The type of questions which are likely to be asked and given serious consideration would be: What is the efficiency of energy conversion? What is the cost per unit of power generation? Is it a safe design? Will it withstand earthquakes? Rarely would a question be asked about the ecological consequences of creating a huge artificial reservoir of water or the social consequences of relocating the populace. And the result is that many multipurpose hydroelectric projects such as the prestigious Aswan High Dam in Egypt, end up as a liability rather than an asset. As has been aptly summed up by Sale[7]: Egypt built that (Aswan Dam) with much fanfare and vast expense in order to provide electricity for its people, increase agricultural production through controlled irrigation, increase fish production by providing a new lake, and thus improve the general standard of living. But the dam has blocked off the Nilewaters so that millions of tons of natural fertilisers end up in the lake behind it and never get either to the farm lands downstream, severely harming agricultural production, or to the marine life of the delta, severely curtailing fish production. So the government planners were forced to use much of the electricity from the dam not for home or industry but to make artificial fertilisers for the farmers and, some day they hope, artificial chemicals for the delta fishermen, thus using electricity to solve the problem created by the dam that was built to solve the problem of electricity! But since the artificial fertilisers so far have been strange to the soil and do not work as well as the natural ones, and since delta waters, stagnant now for much of the year, have bred a variety of diseases, the overall standard of living has in fact been lowered.

As another illustration of the harmful consequences of modern reductionistic technology let us consider the much talked of Green Revolution which, by effecting a manifold increase in food productivity per acre of land, promises to remove food deficiency of the globe. Once again, our tunnelled vision makes us rejoice at the fact that the introduction of high yielding varieties of seeds can more than double the food production, and we even lose sight of the simple economic facts that these high yielding varieties demand besides positive irrigation increasingly larger inputs of fertiliser every year[8], not to speak of caring for long term consequences of dumping of synthetic fertilisers on the soil and surface water. And as is now becoming evident[6], "...this vast elevation in the natural levels of soil nutrients has so stressed the biology of the soil that harmful amounts of nitrate have been introduced into surface waters".

The reductionistic nature of modern technology has also had very serious social consequences. The breaking down of the process of production into a series of specialized operations, each one of which is carried on by a specialized worker has been dubbed as 'monstrous dehumanization' by Mumford[8a]; for, "...It transforms the worker into a cripple, a monster, by forcing him to develop some highly specialized dexterity at the cost of a world of productive impulses and faculties.... To begin with the worker sells his labour power to capital because he himself lacks the material means requisite to the production of a commodity. But now his labour power actually renounces work unless it is sold to capital"[8a]. This dehumanizing aspect is brought out even more glaringly in the modern technology of mass production, and we shall delve into it at length later.

Technology and Centralisation

Another important hallmark of modern technology is the gigantic scale of its operation; for the bigger the scale of operation the lower are the costs per unit of output and thus higher the profits. Economy of scale is the keyword. And a direct consequence of large-scale operation is centralisation?

If economies of scale are really there, why should we grudge bigness of scale? And what, if any, is the relationship of modern maladies to centralisation.

Admittedly, these are difficult questions which may not have unique cut-and -dry answers. Nevertheless, certain general observations can be easily made.

Firstly, these economies of scale, which we often talk about in order to justify mega-technology, are only illusory and appear only because our tubular vision shows us only the direct costs involved in any technology; the hidden costs, e.g. the cost of depleting the non-renewable resources for future generations, the cost of polluting the environment (for example immediate and future costs of acid rain, the damage to the health of miners providing coal for the society, etc.), completely escape our notice. A case of clever book-keeping! Should these costs also be properly apportioned, it is very likely that the concept of 'economy of scale' will be turned turtle.

Nevertheless, the fact remains that modern technology is inherently prone to large-scale operation. There is, for example, no way of economically constructing and running small power stations (based on modern technology) for individual villages. Consequently, the moment we think of meeting the energy needs of villages in a developing nation like India, we have to enter the groove of rural electrification, leading ultimately to a centralised power station—thermal or nuclear, as the case may be—located scores of miles away from the village. Modern power generation technology is an excellent example which demonstrates the inbuilt 'centralising' character of modern technology. Throughout the world, and especially in India, we notice that the current trend is towards super-thermal power stations generating over 1000 MW at one station and feeding a vast territory through a maze of distribution lines. And this malaise of large-scale 'centralised' operation of modern technology is invading deeper and deeper into our lives. In most modern cities, we now boast of centralised supply of even our daily needs like water, milk and bread.

This 'centralising' attitude of modern technology has numerous far-reaching consequences on the society. Thus, setting up of a heavy industry—say a super thermal power station, or a modern steel plant—implies creation of a large number of jobs at one place. In most of the cases, the local populace (which might also have to be relocated) is unable to make use of these job opportunities for they demand high degree of specialised skill. At best, some of them get 'employed' as labourers, while a large number of skilled personnel come from outside. While the protagonists of modern technology would like to view this as a sure means of promoting 'national integration', the reality is often otherwise. The local populace is estranged and feels trampled; social disaffection follows leading often to high crime rates in settlements around industrial establishments. And how good are these settlements? Perhaps some of the worst ever living conditions in the history of modern civilization exist in the shanties which sprawl up around the industrial townships. And whenever the industries are close to a big city—and this is certainly the trend—the labourers and daily wage earners in these industries overflow into the slums of the city making them hot beds of crime and violence. Modern technology has certainly contributed to such maladies as increasing urbanisation and social strife.

Another very deleterious consequence of this 'centralisation-warp' is the increase of social inequity — the widening of gap between the rich and the poor. A study of the social consequences of one of the 'marvels' of modern technology—the Green Revolution—brings out this point rather strikingly[9]. In Punjab (India), (which is one of the great success stories of the Green Revolution), from 1960 to 1968 wheat production in a typical district increased by 300 per cent. And this was accompanied by an increase in the number of large sized farms, which took place by buying out of smaller farms. In twelve years, farms of over twenty acre size expanded in area by 9 per cent. And while there was a net outmigration, during this period the proportion of landless labourers in the male work force increased from 9.2 to 19.8 per cent[9]. While this is the extent to which inequity increased within Punjab as a result of 'Green Revolution', one can easily think about the magnitude of inequity between Punjab and say Bihar, another big state of India where 'Green revolution' has not been 'so successful'.

Quite often this increase of inequity is ascribed to extraneous factors like lack of enthusiasm to new technology, inherent inertia to change, lack of industriousness etc. leading to some farmers, or even regions, not benefiting 'so much' from the new technology. While these factors could definitely have certain effect, the principal reason for this increase of inequity lies in the nature of technology itself. As has been pointed out by Griffin[10], there is an inherent bias in the Green Revolution technology arising from the biological characteristics of the seeds, for "they require an abundant and controlled water supply and hence are most suitable for regions which already enjoy a good irrigation system." This is clearly the main reason for the 'success' of Green Revolution in Punjab, where a well laid-out irrigation system emanating from Bhakhra Dam exists; and its comparative failure elsewhere in India. Moreover, "...this technical change has had a discriminatory impact because the new varieties are intensive in their use of material inputs, especially fertiliser...."[10] Naturally, farmers with small land holdings, having very little purchasing power are unable to provide these intensive material inputs with the result that they are labelled 'unprogressive' and ultimately get squeezed out. The bigger units, on the other hand, can comparatively easily afford to provide increased fertiliser inputs and thus 'demonstrate' themselves to be more 'efficient'. Of course, Government policies, the policies of financial institutions do also play a major role in 'growth/curtailment' of social inequity. Nevertheless this 'demonstrable' efficiency of larger farms always makes lending organizations believe that smaller units are just not viable with the result that large producers are often able to dominate financial resources too. A vicious circle thus sets in with big farms growing continuously bigger and slowly transforming smaller farmers into landless labourers[11].

Yet another direct consequence of the promotion of 'bigness' is the phenomenal increase in environmental pollution. As has also been pointed out by Schumacher[12], "small–scale operations, no matter how numerous, are always less likely to be harmful to the natural environment than large-scale ones, simply because their individual force is small in relation to the recuperative forces of nature". Thus elaborate pollution control gadgets are required in thermal power plants, not because they are the only users of coal, but because their intensity of burning of coal is so large that the resultant flue gases cannot naturally diffuse in the environment without causing harmful concentrations of poisonous gases. Or, consider the problem of water pollution arising from improper sewage disposal in cities. The pollution of river Yamuna during its 48 km stretch passing through Delhi is illustrative of its magnitude. Everyday, the river picks up nearly 200 million litres of untreated sewage, besides 20 million litres of industrial effluents (including about half a million litres of DDT wastes), with the result that from Delhi to Agra (about 150 km stretch) the Yamuna water is unfit for drinking and bathing[13]. Why should so much of untreated sewage flow into the river? Mainly because the only concept that modern technology accepts for sewage disposal is that of big centralised units which are highly capital intensive. The alternative decentralised concept of sewage disposal at the source (e.g., through properly designed septic tanks etc.), which can easily eliminate this pollution altogether, seem to be an anathema to modern technology.

Another implication of 'centralised' heavy technologies, which is likely to assume more and more serious proportions, is their massive potential of causing harm in the event of any accident and/or sabotage. The death of over two thousand people and disability of over hundred thousand people due to the gas leak in Bhopal is a serious warning of things to come. One can imagine the far-reaching consequences of a similar leak in a nuclear power station and only pray that such a thing does not occur! But the fact remains that this 'risk' is an integral part of 'centralised' technologies.

Technology and Mass Production

One of the key factors responsible for great commercial success of modern technology is mass production, especially though automation. An authoritative enunciation of the objectives of automation makes this point quite clear: "...the objectives of automation are to reduce manufacturing costs by increasing productivity, and to improve product quality and reliability by reducing or eliminating human errors"[14]. Further, since 'to err is human', the best way to eliminate human errors—and thus improve product quality and reliability—is to eliminate the human operator altogether! The cherished utopia of modern industrial estate is, therefore, a factory run entirely by robots ensuring highest product quality and reliability at the lowest possible costs—a dream likely to be realised soon in the 'developed' nations.

The damaging results of this ethos of modern technology are already surfacing, especially in the heavily industrialised parts of the world. Besides fanning the already raging fires of consumerism, automation is one of the main factors responsible for worldwide increase in unemployment. Though the advocates of automation often mention that it only changes the structure of employment from blue-collared jobs to white-collared jobs and that the redundant labour could be easily absorbed by the alternative employment opportunities so created, this is only true in theory. As has been pointed out [15], "...the labour supply is not elastic, and its rigidity is intensified by the emergence of new skills. All these factors create unemployment, which is accentuated by the accelerating speed of economic change,.... In particular, older and unskilled workers, racial minority groups, or even new entrants may be at serious disadvantage". Thus, in fact, automation creates unemployment for that strata of society, which needs employment the most. And with the creation of an ethos of scorn for physical labour, we have the strange paradox of unemployment existing side by side with jobs in many industrialised societies.

Another very serious consequence of the mass production technologies, to which many industrial psychologists have repeatedly drawn attention, is their dehumanizing influence on the workers. Often, modern technology is hailed as the Great Deliverer, which has relieved mankind from toil and drudgery. Unfortunately this relieving seems to have gone too far! In the attempt to improve the work efficiency and reduce the expenditure of physical energy, the tasks in a modern industry have been simplified to such an extent that they demand little skill and knowledge, thus giving hardly any job-satisfaction to the workers. An analysis of the tasks of workers 'tied' to an assembly line in an automobile industry serves to illustrate this point. Consider, for example, the job of the automotive worker who installs toeplates[16] :

"I put in the two different toeplates that cover the holes where the brake and clutch pedals are. I am inside the car and have to be down on the seat to do my work. On one kind of car I put in the shift lever while another man puts in the toeplates."

The sense of achievement which this worker would have at the end of a shift can be easily imagined. And the above description of his work, gives only half the story. The extent of 'pressure' under which he has to work and the repetitiveness and monotony of job can be gauged from the additional information provided by Walker[16], who carried out this study :

> "While doing his job this man rides along in the car performing two operations, and must complete the job in 2 minutes, or else he will be carried too far. He then returns to his station, climbs into another car, and begins all over again. Thus his pace is strictly governed by the moving line. Such a job is also highly repetitive.... The job demands very little skill and has a learning period of just 2 days. Although the worker gets in and out of car 20 or 30 times an hour, his expenditure of physical energy on the actual operation is slight".

As corroborated by Walker, a somewhat similar situation applies to jobs not on a moving belt. In fact, this lack of clear identification with a particular job, repetitive nature of tasks, extreme pressure of work demanding unremitting attention which leaves little scope for interpersonal interaction are common features of all modern industries. The result, in concise words of Pius XI[17] : *From the factory dead matter goes out improved, whereas men there are corrupted and degraded'*. The complete *meaninglessness of work* thus seems to be a *necessary outcome of modern* mass-production *technology*.

And what does this lead to? When work loses meaning and ceases to be a source of satisfaction, man searches for these elsewhere—in alcohol, in drugs, in sex, in aggressive behaviour etc. If a survey were to be conducted of job-wise distribution of alcoholics in any society, factory workers would definitely top the list. In fact, it has now been even 'scientifically' established that mental health is directly related to the nature of job. Says Kornhauser on the basis of a substantial study conducted over several years: "When we compare the factory workers by occupational categories, the higher the occupation (in respect to skill and associated attributes of variety, responsibility and pay) the better the mental health. Those in skilled jobs have highest mental-health scores, followed by the semiskilled and, lowest of all, the men in routine, repetitive types of work.[18]" Certainly, modern technology cannot claim credit for promoting 'skill'. The mass production ethic, in fact, has been the singular factor responsible for decline of traditional skills, forcing 'enlightened' societies to 'preserve' mastercraftsmen as 'rare species' on verge of extinction!

This dehumanizing nature of work has some very subtle effects which have far-reaching consequences on the society for our approach to 'work' is closely related to our approach to life itself. As beautifully put by Wright Mills[19], " *as work declines in meaning and gives no inner direction or center, leisure becomes the end of life itself*, and the leisure ethic swallows up all values, including those of work". Often, increase in the leisure time available is cited as one of the main benefits of modern technology, in the hope that relieved from his continued pre-occupation with satisfying material needs, man will be able to devote himself to truly humane activities—to creative arts, music, painting, philosophy,—to self-cultivation in short. This again appears perfect in theory, but fails miserably in practice,—as is borne out by the state of modern civilisation. A man who spends a major portion of his waking hours in meaningless, debasing work cannot be expected to, and does not, switch over to meaningful creative activities during the leisure time. His sensibilities are too stultified to respond to his own higher needs, and the mass production of distraction—through round-the-clock radio and TV programmes, media and advertising which are, in the words of Wright Mills[19], as much a part of the (technological) way of life as the mass production of automobiles—does not give him much freedom over his leisure-time. The unity of work and leisure, which has been known from very ancient times to be the prerequisite for a purposeful existence of human beings is totally alien to modern mass production technology. This subtle factor must definitely be contributing its share to the erosion of human values, which is the prime malady affecting modern society.

Technology and Wastefulness

Though it may appear paradoxical at first—for modern technology lays so much premium on efficiency, productivity and value analysis, —it is incontrovertible that modern technological culture promotes waste, and that too of the most precious endowment of mankind, viz., the non-renewable resources like minerals, fossil fuels etc. This again happens due to certain characteristics which are absolutely intrinsic to it, and is not an incidental by-product of technology.

Firstly, waste directly follows from the ethic of 'abundance' which is fundamental to modern technology, for it is 'normal' for human societies to be careless about the usage of commodities existing in abundance. And quite often, this 'abundance' is only illusory. For example, by making water and electricity available at the turn of a knob, modern technology fosters an illusion in the minds of the users of their inexhaustible availability, promoting their wasteful usage. How otherwise can one explain the fact that with every stroke of flush latrines in a city 20 litres of filtered water are thrown into sewer without any compunction? Or, the fact that buildings are so designed that even when the sun is shining bright outside we need illumination inside the building? Such wastefulness is almost non-existent in sections of society which are still not 'benefitting' from modern technology, e.g., in villages in India where water has to be drawn out from wells or through hand pumps it is still treated as a precious commodity, and soon after installation of a tube well, the culture of waste starts overtaking.

Waste also follows from another 'natural' outcome of the ethic of abundance, viz., discarding commodities much before their useful life is over. The pressure of advertising, and quite often manufacturing policies of companies regarding spares of their 'old' products, literally force the consumers to change over to the 'new-model' or the 'new-fashion'. This situation has reached alarming proportions in the affluent societies. The bicycles that can last twenty-five years are actually used in the U.S. for an average of only two years; industrial equipment that could go for twenty years is actually used for an average of twelve years; soda bottles that can have a useful life of five years actually last for about ninety-three days and cars that can easily last ten years are in fact replaced every 2.2 years[20]. The result, U.S.A. creates something like 3 billion tons of solid waste material every year[21], justifying its epithet of acme of 'throw-away' society. And what does this garbage consist of? Precious metals like iron, aluminium and copper whose reserves are dwindling fast. Incredible though it may appear, according to Professor Earl Cook in quarterly *Technology Review* : "some municipal dumps have higher percentage of copper than some mines that are operated profitably right now in the Rockies".[22]

What is most unfortunate is that this ethic of wastefulness is now being accepted as a legitimate engineering design practice, as is borne out by the following extract from a reputed engineering handbook[23] :

> The concept of reliability has been broadened and changed in the past two decades...so that the designer is not always striving for long life. Indeed, many of the very complex systems now being designed are intended to operate for only a short period of time, with a primary requirement being that no failure occurs during this short operating period. Consequently, designing for long operating life will not be here considered.

Consequently, purposeful design for product failure is no longer considered unethical. 'Design for Planned Obsolescence' is now openly discussed as a pragmatic philosophy. There are already portents that we are moving towards the Cornucopia City of Packard[24] :

> In Cornucopia City, as I understand it, all the buildings will be made of a special papier-mache. These houses can be torn down and rebuilt every spring and fall at house

> cleaning time. The motor cars of Cornucopia will be made of a lightweight plastic that develops fatigue and begins to melt if driven more than four thousand miles. Owners who turn in their old motor cars at the regular turn-in dates—New Year day, Easter, Independence Day, and Labour Day—will be rewarded with a one-hundred dollar United States Prosperity-through-Growth Bond for each motor car turned in.... One-fourth of the factories of Cornucopia City will be located on the edge of a cliff, and the ends of their assembly lines can be swung to the front or rear doors depending upon the public demand for the product being produced. When demand is slack, the end of the assembly line will be swung to the rear door out of sight and go directly to their graveyard without first overwhelming the consumer market.

Waste, especially of energy, is also an inescapable outcome of centralisation, which as discussed above, is a fundamental characteristic of modern technology. Nowhere is this so evident, as in the rapidly growing Food Processing industry. Rifkin[25], for example, identifies seventeen energy-consuming operations which are necessary before the English muffin can reach the break–fast tables in United States, and concludes"....Not only have tens of thousands of energy calories gone into the entire process, but medical evidence suggests that both the additives and the lack of fiber in refined breads may pose a serious hazards to health.... Of the total amount of energy used in the food system, less than 20 per cent actually goes into the growing of food. The other 80 per cent is consumed by the processing, packaging, distribution, and preparation of the foodstuff"[25]. The rapidly growing frozen food technology is another serious culprit, in so far as the energy wastage is concerned. The food product is first heated (process is called blanching, and its purpose is to destroy certain enzymes which would otherwise give off flavours during long-term storage); then cooled and frozen, held in frozen stores, transported in refrigerated vans, only to be heated again by the consumer before eating.

And of course, we also have energy consumption in various other 'processing' operations which are necessary to ensure 'proper quality' product (Fig. 2).

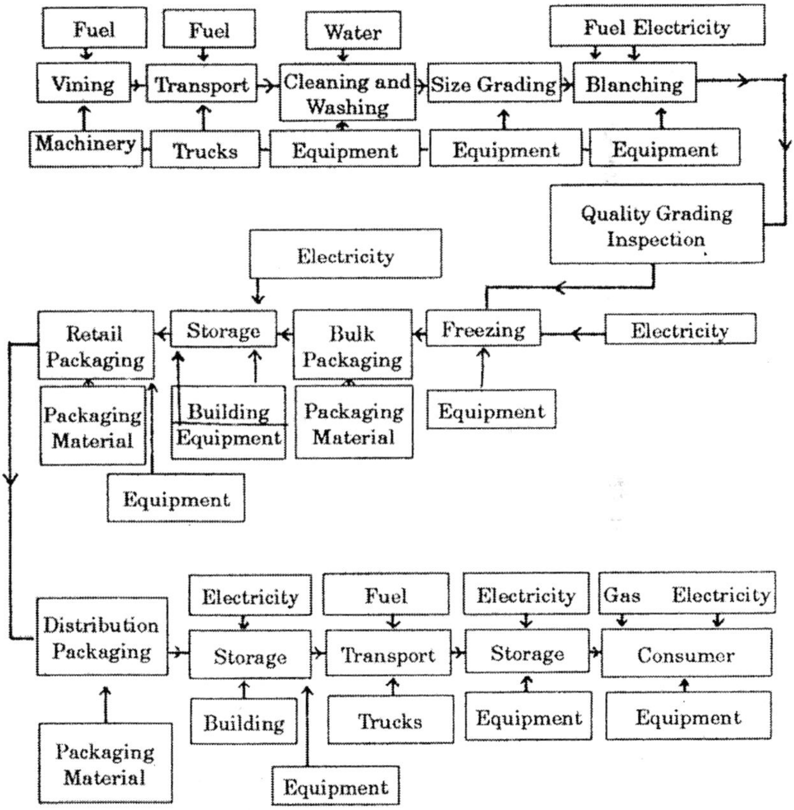

Fig.2 Frozen-Peas Food Chain

The extent of wastage of energy (and materials) which thus arises can be easily gauged by looking at Fig. 2 wherein, as an illustration, the various operations involved in consumption of 'garden-peas' via the frozen-food technology are enumerated. The contrast between this mode and the 'primitive' method of eating fresh garden-peas is too evident to demand any detailed explanation.

Technology and Self-Reliance

Modern technology is often hailed as the only tool available for promoting self-reliance, both at the level of an individual and at the collective national level. Thus developing nations quickly embrace modern technology in the hope that it will free them from dependence on other countries for their very basic requirements of food and consumer goods. Again, within every society individuals vie with each other to usurp the fruits of technology in order to be 'independent'. A closer scrutiny however reveals that this 'independence' or 'self-reliance' is only illusory. A fundamental characteristic of modern technology which reveals itself is its total dependence on complex socio-technical support systems needed not only during manufacture, but also during use and maintenance of its products. A few examples will bring out this point clearly.

Let us first consider the much talked of 'self-reliance' in food having been achieved by developing nations like India by the use of modern technology. It is clear that food production in India has increased appreciably over last two decades and that it has been possible to stop food imports. But that does not automatically imply 'self-reliance' for in order to achieve and sustain this level of food production, India is totally dependent on import of synthetic fertilisers. As has been pointed out[28], in India before the Green Revolution, expenditure on imports of agricultural requisites was almost nil, in 1950-51, it amounted to just 70 million rupees; in 1970-71, this had risen to Rs. 1020 million and in 1974-75 the expenditure on fertilizer import alone stood at Rs. 5325 million. And if the imports required to build up indigenous capacity in fertilizers and agricultural machinery are also counted, it becomes quite clear that far from making the country self-reliant in food, the dependence of agricultural sector on foreign inputs has infact increased multifold.*

The same is true of other modern technological products. Whether it be the telephone or the automobile, their very operation demands complicated support systems extending far away from the users. Often these dependencies are so much obscured that special effort has to be made to be even aware of them, but these nevertheless exist. This was dramatically demonstrated in the case of automobile during 1973-74 by the Arab oil embargo. And in so far as modern communication technology is concerned, the extreme dependence of users on unknown faces—bordering often on helplessness—is an everyday experience, at least in countries like India. Even in such a crucial sector like energy, virtually no country in the world can claim to be self-reliant. The oil-exporting countries have to be dependent on others for the gadgets to consume the 'abundant' oil and those capable of producing these gadgets are often at the mercy of the former to get the oil to 'run' them!

It must be clarified here that there is fundamentally nothing wrong with 'dependence' per se. In fact, a technology which demands the cooperation of a number of people for its usage could become an agent for furthering mutual cooperation and other related human values in society. Interdependence could be promotive or contrient to cooperation depending on whether the people are interdependent in such a way that each individual's progress towards the shared goal helps or prevents the other people in achieving the goal[29]. Clearly modern technology creates interdependence between sets of people who may even be totally unaware of each other (e.g., telephone users and the operators.), who have hardly any shared goal (especially in view of the prevailing materialistic worldview) with the result that it does not and cannot

*This aspect has rather dramatically manifested itself in our country recently when, after 4 decades of extensive industrialization, we were forced to mortgage our gold reserves in order to pay the *interest* on the foreign debts!

lead to any desirable consequence. Neither does modern technology promote 'self-reliance' nor co-operation through interdependence.

Technology and Social Problems

Modern technology not only accentuates some grave social maladies as discussed above, but also obscures the social roots of many serious problems of our times with the result that technological solutions are sought to alleviate these. This often results in exacerbating the problem as the real causes remain unmitigated. A few examples will elucidate this point.

Consider the problem of increasing crime and terrorism—so evident now in all 'developing' (and of course, in 'developed') nations including India. The technological perception of this problem results in a strategy to combat it by increasing sophistication of the arms and equipment available with police, thus relegating to background the root causes which may be increasing inequity, alienation of a segment of society etc.

Or, take the problem of population explosion. Viewed with 'technological glasses' it is sought to be solved through better technologies for birth control. Its real roots—economic and old-age insecurity of masses, general increase in sexual indulgence due to lack of creative outlets of human endeavour—are often pushed into the background. Similarly, 'Energy Crisis' propels us to search for alternative sources of energy and nobody seems to question our unending 'greed' for 'goods' and 'services' beyond those necessary for convivial living. The question, 'How much energy does a man need?' is never raised.* Housing shortage has the only solution of constructing more and more houses (ranging from skyscrapers to mudhouses) and the fact that disintegration of families is causing a phenomenal increase in the demand for houses

---

*probably for the fear of getting a reply similar to that given by Tolstoy to the question, 'How much land does a man need?'

is totally overlooked. Even corruption in offices is sought to be eliminated by 'computerisation' and a reign of 'truth' established by eliminating lies via 'lie-detectors'!

Needless to add, the solution strategies based on a purely technological perception only aggravate the problem. Introduction of sophisticated arms in police has only spurred the criminals to improve their weaponry resulting in an increase in crime, construction of more and more houses has only increased the attraction of people towards cities exacerbating urbanisation and the housing shortage, and development of 'safe' birth control devices has only increased licentious living and we have the 'side effects' of sexually transmitted diseases like AIDS.*

Conclusions

The above discussion clearly establishes that modern technology is intrinsically unsuitable to serve as an instrument of progress. Most of the modern maladies, viz., environmental pollution, nuclear armament, increasing strife and violence, urbanisation, increasing inequity, etc. have been created and/or are being further fueled by modern technology. This is not just because of any aberrations or errors of judgement in applying the technology, but as brought out by Fig. 3, a natural outcome of its fundamental characteristics — its genetic code. In fact, the very characteristics which are responsible for its phenomenal 'success' and popularity are also basically responsible for these technogenic and social maladies (Figure 3), some of which even threaten the whole civilization itself. The obvious conclusion which thus emerges is that for happy survival of mankind on the 'spaceship-earth' we need an altogether different brand of technology—a humanistic technology—which is based on a correct understanding of human welfare. The modern technology has been evolved in a materialistic worldview which equates

---

* which unfortunately are sought to be mitigated only through development of AIDS vaccine.

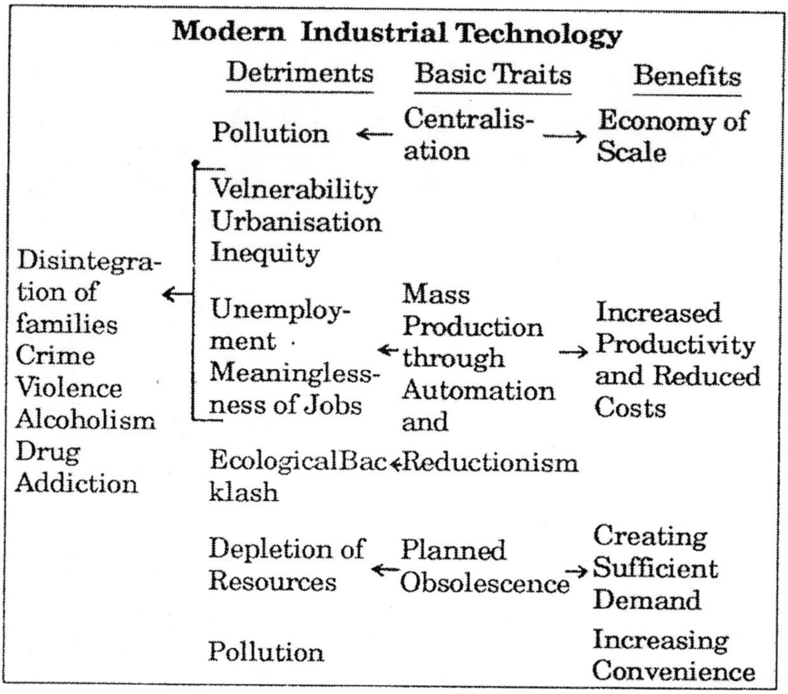

Fig. 3

human welfare with material-prosperity, and the consequences are before us. Thus, purely on the basis of empirical evidence we can now say that materialistic philosophy is incongruent with true human welfare. It is not that thinkers and philosophers in the past were ignorant of this. Even during the heydays of industrial revolution, when the society was inebriated with the idea of progress through technology, there were people who questioned the materialistic world view and the industrial technology, the most prominent amongst them being Mahatma Gandhi, the father of the Indian Nation. With the insight of a visionary, he was able to see through the dangers of industrialisation and pointed these out in his seminal work '*Hind Swaraj*' written in 1909[30]. Gandhi repeatedly stressed the point that 'evils are inherent in industrialism' in his protracted (but little known) debate with Pandit Nehru on the strategy for the development of India after independence. But such was the sweeping power of the prevalent paradigm, and the attraction of the 'immediate gains' obtainable through industrialisation that, to quote Pandit Nehru[31], 'Few of us, I think, accepted Gandhiji's old ideas about machinery and modern civilization. We thought that even he looked upon them as utopian and as largely inapplicable to modern conditions'. The result: India also went for rapid industrialisation and all the aforementioned problems are slowly assuming alarming proportions.

A question naturally arises in the mind:

How is it that this materialistic worldview got so firmly entrenched in the society; as it is known for certain that right from Ancient world down to Middle Ages, the prevailing worldview spurned material accumulation as positive hindrance to 'salvation', which was the sole purpose of life? How is it that this legacy of two millennia was overthrown in less than two centuries?

Our journey to the pinnacle of materialism, which is a very interesting and educative study, shall be the subject of next Chapter.

NOTES

1. Gerald Piel, quoted in *Technology and Human Values* by Watkins, B.O. and Roy Meador, Ann Arbor Science, Mich, 1977; p. 101.
2. Melvin Kranzberg, quoted in *Technology and Human Values*, ibid.
3. Mumford Lewis, *Technics and Civilization*, Routledge and Kegan Paul Ltd., London, 1934, p. 153.
4. Galbraith, J.K., *The New Industrial State*, New American Library, New York, 1967, p. 24.
5. Reductionism is the view that effective understanding of a real, complex system can be achieved by investigating the properties of its isolated parts. A holistic view would be that which demands an understanding of reality in terms of integrated wholes whose properties cannot be fully deduced from those of smaller units.
6. Commoner, Bary : 'On the Meaning of Ecological Failures in International Development' in *The Careless Technology–Ecology and International Development*, Edited by M.T. Farvar and J.P. Milton, the Natural History Press, Garden City, New York, 1972.
7. Sale, Kirkpatrick : *Human Scale*, Coward, McCann and Geoghegan, New York, 1980, p 30.

   This book contains a well researched account of the dangers of growth mania, amply illustrated with facts and figures from authentic sources. The need for scaling down of our present institutions to what he calls, the 'human scale' is forcefully brought out.
8. Kirkpatrick Sale (ref. 7 above, p. 229) quotes from authentic U.S. Statistics that:

   (a) From 1940 to 1975 US farm output increased by 90 per cent, while fertiliser use increased by about 900 per cent.

   (b) In 1949, some 11,000 tons of fertiliser nitrogen were used in the US per unit of crop production. In 1968, some 57,000 tons were used to produce the same yield, and in 1975, some 95,000 tons.

8a. Mumford, Lewis, op.cit., p 146.

9. Meadows, Donnella : "Equity, the Free Market and the Sustainable state", Chapter 7 in *Alternatives to Growth*, Ed. Dennis L. Meadows, Bollinger Publishing Co. Cambridge, Massachusetts. 1977.
10. Griffin, Keith : *The Political Economy of Agrarian Change*, Macmillan, London, 1978, p. 52.
11. Bajaj, J.K. : "Green Revolution : A Historical Perspective", *PPST Bulletin*, Vol 2, No 2, Nov. 1982.

The paper gives an interesting account of the consequences of Green Revolution in India, especially of disparties created due to this.

12. Schumacher, E.F. : *Small is Beautiful*, Abacus, London, 1947, p. 29.

    This, now classic book by Schumacher brings out very cogently the basic flaws in the Western concept of unabated growth as a panacea for all human misery. Schumacher coined the term 'Intermediate-technology' for the type of technology which, in his opinion, is best suited for development, especially of the Third World countries having meagre resources.

13. *The State of India's Environment 1982 —A Citizen's Report*, Centre for Science and Environment, New Delhi, 1982, p. 20.

14. Dallas, D.B. (Ed.) *Tool and Manufacturing Engineers Handbook*, (Third Ed.), McGraw Hill, NY, 1976, pp. 12–2.

15. Rose, J : *Automation–Its uses and consequences*, Oliver and Boyd, London, 1967, p. 67.

16. Walker, C.R. : "Basic Human Problems in Mass-Production Technologies : Pacing, Pressure and Repetitiveness", p. 95–102 in *Technology, Industry, and Man–the Age of Acceleration* by C.R. Walker, McGraw Hill, NY. 1968.

17. Pius Xi quoted in Schumacher, op. cit., p. 29.

18. Kornhauser, Arthur, cited in Walker, C.R. op. cit., p 101.

19. C. Wright Mills : "The Unity of Work and Leisure", p. 420-423 in *Proper Study of Man*, J. Fadiman (Ed.), MacMillan, NY, 1971.

20. Sale, Kirkpatrick, op.cit., p. 90.

21. ibid., p. 243.

22. Cited in Sale, ibid., p 247.

23. Rothbart, H.A. (Ed.) : *Mechanical Design and Systems Handbook*, McGraw Hill, NY, 1964, p 18–37.

24. Packard Vance : *The Waste Makers*, David Mckay Company Inc., NY., 1960.

25. Rifkin, J. and T. Howard : *Entropy – A New World View*. The Viking Press, New York, 1980, p 131–132.

26. Londahl, G. "Energy Cost Analysis and Energy Savings", in *Proceedings XV* Intl. Congress of Refrigeration, Venice, 1979 Vol. IV, pp. 29–35.

27. Mumford, Lewis, op. cit., p. 185.

28. Bajaj, J.K., op. cit., pp. 102–103.

29. Berkowitz, L. "*A Survey of Social Psychology*", Holt, Rinehart and Winston, N.Y. Sec. Ed., 1980, p 410.

30. Gandhi, M.K., *Hind Swaraj*, 1909 (Reprinted by Navjivan Publishing House).

A seminal work wherein Gandhi outlines the full import of his concept of Swaraj; and probably the earliest critique of modern industrial technology. It constituted the basic framework for all of Gandhi's future life and activities.

31. *PPST Bulletin*, "What is Development : Recalling an Old Debate", Vol. 3, No. 1, May 1983, pp. 3–11. PPST Group, Madras.

3 DEVELOPMENT OF MATERIALISTIC WORLD-VIEW

If we find that the ascertainment of the order of nature is facilitated by using one terminology or one set of symbols, rather than another, it is our clear duty to use the former; and no harm can accrue, so long as we bear in mind that we are dealing merely with terms and symbols....

But the man of science who, forgetting the limits of philosophical inquiry slides from these formulas and symbols into what is commonly understood by materialism, seems to me to place himself on a level with the mathematician who should mistake the x's and the y's with which he works his problems for real entities, and with this further disadvantage, as compared with the mathematician, that the blunders of the latter are of no practical consequence while the errors of systematic materialism may paralyse the energies and destroy the beauty of a life.

Thomas Huxley
Methods and Results

In the present stage of evolution of homo sapiens, the psyche seems to be so much tuned to seeking pleasant sensations that it is believed to be a perfectly 'normal' propensity of man to maximise sense gratification. Consequently, the materialistic worldview – the belief that happiness lies solely in material accumulation and resulting sense enjoyments — is so tenaciously entrenched in the society that most people find it difficult even to visualise that any alternative is possible. Yet, it is a historical fact that even in the west, the worldview before sixteenth century—during the so-called middle ages—was much different. It is difficult to coin a phrase which would concisely indicate its main distinguishing features; and for want of a better word, we shall use Rifkin's phrase, 'Christian Worldview' to denote it; for during the entire millennium with which we identify middle ages(1), Christianity and church exerted a very strong influence on the western mind. The roots of this worldview are to be found in the teachings of ancient Greek philosophers Socrates and Plato who preceded Jesus, for the early fathers of the church were strongly influenced by Platonic thought, besides, of course, the message of Jesus as communicated by his teachings and exemplary life. A study of the development of materialistic worldview should thus rightfully begin with a brief introduction to Socratic–Platonic thought, especially because it brings out in stark contrast the differences between the two paradigms.

Socratic–Platonic Thought

Socrates, Greek sage and philosopher of fifth century B.C., was in fact the harbinger of a silent revolt against the cult of 'successful living' based entirely on material possessions, which was so prevalent in ancient Greece. As has been indicated by Mumford(2), though the Greek society was crassly materialistic, nevertheless the inevitable disillusionment with power and material wealth was also creeping in. "The ruling classes constantly were enervated by the surfeit of goods and pleasures they had so ruthlessly monopolized for themselves. They had lapsed, too many of these insolent rulers and their agents, from a human to a distinctly simian level: like the apes, they snatched food for themselves, instead of sharing it with the group: like them, too, the more powerful claimed more than their share of women : like them, again, they were in a constant state of nettled aggression toward possible rivals. In short, they had alienated themselves from their distinctly human potentialities...."

During such an era, Socrates, through the example of his own plain and simple life and through his powerful precepts epitomised the revolt against all the pomps and vanities of 'worldly success' which degraded humanity and shrivelled the spirit. Being a practical philosopher he concerned himself primarily with the question of human happiness. He taught: happiness does not depend on external physical goods and luxurious life, but on knowingly acting rightly. Man's true fortune is to be sought in virtue alone, and Socrates believed that true virtue consists in right knowing, which always leads to right acting, for "If a man has real knowledge of virtue, that is, if he truly sees the Idea of Virtue, he is virtuous, for nobody having attained such pure knowledge can do wrong readily"[(6)]. This maxim, often termed the Socratic Doctrine of Identity of virtue and knowledge formed the core of his teaching.

This 'right knowledge', or what we may term as 'insight' or wisdom, which should be free from all errors of perception and opinion, was thus in a sense equated with the knowledge of the 'Good'. Socrates himself did not indicate how to obtain this 'right knowledge' though he did identify certain important virtues such as obedience of law, suffering wrong rather than doing wrong and most important of all, self-control. It is only through the writings of his students, especially Plato, that we get a clearer idea of their thinking on what constitutes 'Good'.

In his quest for an unequivocal answer to this question, Plato was led to conclude that 'right knowledge' could not be obtained through sense perception, for the 'sensible world'– the world which we perceive by our senses—is transient, continually changing and subject to decay, ageing and death. About this world, there can only be certain opinion, no definite knowledge, which he suggested could only be obtained by access to the 'super sensible-world', the world of knowledge and ideas, which has permanence and fixity, and is therefore free from all possibilities of errors of perception and judgement. The ideas which constitute this super-sensible world (in contrast to objects which constitute the sensible world) are incorporeal and quite obviously cannot be grasped by the senses, but only by thought, by 'divine contemplations'. The Idea of Good, the wisdom, also belongs to this super-sensible world, and in Plato's own words[(5)] : "... in the world of knowledge, the idea of good seen, is also inferred to be the Universal author of all things beautiful and right...the immediate source of reason and truth...and that this is the power upon which he who would act rationally either in public or private life must have his eye fixed".

In Plato's philosophy we thus find a consummation of Socratic teachings. Socrates taught: True happiness—the perfect realisation of one's 'being'—needs right action which in turn demanded 'right knowledge'. This knowledge could dawn only with a clear understanding of the idea of 'Good' and Plato indicated that 'divine contemplation' of the super-sensible world would reveal the idea of 'Good'. Perfection of man thus necessitated a knowledge of super-sensible realities and accordingly, in his *Academy* too, Plato laid emphasis on 'enlightening' his students, on creating in them a love of knowledge and of wisdom rather than on imparting any special skill. The ideal of the teachers as also of the students was alike—the search for knowledge is the greatest purification[(6)].

We thus find that Platonic philosophy is a complete antithesis of the materialistic worldview. Like Socrates, he derided all attempts at finding happiness in the 'sensible world', which he likened to the shadow-world of the prisoners of an underground cave who, never having seen anything other than the shadows on the wall of their cave, mistake those shadows for reality. True happiness lay in coming out of this 'prison house' of the 'world of sight' and wilfully undertaking the journey into the intellectual world—quite akin to the journey of those prisoners out of the cave. This, he believed, was the real purpose of a truly human life; seeking sensual delights behoved only brutes.

The Christian Worldview

Plato's philosophy was too 'other worldly' to be acceptable in his own time—and even his own students found some of his concepts too 'idealistic'. Nevertheless, his thought exerted considerable influence on the early fathers of the church and through them on the Christian Worldview which dominated the Western world for over a millennia. In fact, Plato's thoughts were wafted into even more super-rational heights by Neo-Platonists, notable amongst them being Plotinus who enshrined more and more mystical ideas in the philosophy. Numerous doctrines of Plato ,e.g., his doctrine of two worlds were readily accepted in Christian theology, largely by way of St. Paul, Origen and St. Augustine. Thus both Christianity and Neo-Platonism held that ultimate reality of the Universe is not the world of senses which we perceive, but the spirit. The human purpose was not to 'achieve things' but to seek salvation:

> Take heed, and beware of all covetousness
> For a man's life does not consist
> In the abundance of his possessions
> ...Do not be anxious about your life
> What you shall eat or what you shall drink;
> But seek first God's kingdom and his righteousness,
> And all these things shall be yours as well.
> ...The kingdom of God does not mean food and drink,
> But righteousness and peace and joy in the Holy Spirit.[7]

In impressing upon his followers, the absolute importance of virtue and righteousness, Jesus again reiterated Platonic thought and gave it the sanction of his authority. Failure to do what is right was termed as sin:

> Whoever knows what is right to do and fails to do it
> For him it is sin [8].

During the entire span of Middle ages, when Christianity had a dominant role to play in the Western world, with propagation of such teachings the worldview which developed was certainly anti-materialistic. In fact, the world of sight, the perceptible world had little conceptual hold on mind. The activities of daily life had no relevance in themselves, their only significance was in so far as they aided

Man's pilgrimage through eternity. Thus, private luxury was not looked upon with favour, for by promoting covetousness it could be a hindrance to salvation. Gold, ornaments and jewels could only belong to The Virgin for she was the Queen of Heaven; or to other representatives of the divine powers, viz., the King, Queen and Pope. Rather than grabbing and acquiring, giving charity and sharing were preached, and to a large extent practised, as the true virtues:

> Blessed are those who shall hear me say–
> I was hungry and you gave me food,
> I was thirsty and you gave me drink,
> ...
> For truly as you do it to one of the least of these my brethren,
> You do it to me[8].

It would, of course, be presumptuous to say that during the Middle Ages the western society was a biblical utopia, but certainly the influence of Christianity and its worldview was very profound. In the beginning, the Roman Empire brandished Christians as heretics and the early Christians had to face persecution and even death for defying the 'state Gods'. Many were thrown into prison and many torn to pieces by wild animals before jeering crowds in amphitheatres. But the Christians faced humiliation and martyrdom with such confidence that the people began to think that their religion must be true. Slowly, their numbers increased, they were granted religious toleration and in the fourth century A.D., after emperor Constantine embraced Christianity, it became the state religion of the Roman Empire. The fall of Rome to barbarians only strengthened the authority of the church, for it was the only institution capable of preventing total anarchy. The Christian monastries—especially those started by St. Benedict — made a deep impression on the minds of the barbarians, for they could see for themselves that man could really live a blissful life after renouncing all worldly pleasures. Gradually the barbarians 'softened' and even their leaders were attracted to Christianity. Consequently, during the early middle ages, the cordiality between the rulers and the church deepened to such an extent that the church acquired an almost independent status governing the spiritual life quite at par with the political state which governed the secular life. This medieval worldview has been beautifully summed up by historians Magoffin and Duncalf[11], "God has fixed in the firmament two great lights : one to light the day and the other the night. He has also established two powers: one, which is the lesser, to rule over bodies; the other which is the greater, to rule over souls; and just as the moon gets its light from the Sun, so the royal power receives its splendour from the authority lodged in the Pope". Thus, it would not be wrong to say that during the Middle Ages, the Christian worldview prevailed in the Western world. The very possibility of crusades is an indicator of the tremendous hold of church on the populace as well as the kings. This influence can be seen even in such 'worldly matters' like the organisation of medieval guilds. From 12th century onwards, most of the medieval guilds were also directly responsible for acts of charity and succour and fellowship. And as mentioned by Ellul[9], even "technical activity did not escape Christian moral judgement. The question: 'Is it righteous?' was asked of every attempt to change mode of production or organisation. That something might be useful or profitable to men did not make it right and just. It had to fit a precise conception of justice before God. When an element of technique appeared to be righteous from every point of view, it was adopted, but even then with excessive caution... only inventions judged worthy were applied or even allowed to become known".

The Change Over

A belief system which has been the ideal of a society for over a millennium cannot be shaken off like the proverbial flipping of a coin. It is only when the torchbearers of the belief fail to live up to their own precepts that a disenchantment sets in the populace. This is precisely what happened towards the later medieval period and people's faith in the 'Christian worldview' was gradually eroded. Numerous factors contributed to this. Thus, as Christianity grew, so did the ecclesiastical organisation, and the emphasis on secular affairs. The spiritual activity shrank as the church satisfied itself with the role of an absolute mediator between God and Man. This absolute authority made it wealthy and powerful, but also brought in its wake conflicts. The wealth became the cause of its conflicts with the kings and the power brought in internecine confrontation between cardinals. The acme of this degeneration was probably reached in fourteenth century when the believers were faced with the unenviable task of choosing between two Popes each with his own college of cardinals and each claiming the right to rule the whole church![11]

This schism greatly weakened the church for not only did it divide the people into two camps, it also incipiated a questioning of the role of church. And though in 1417 the council of Constance ended the schism after 39 years, people's faith had by then been thoroughly shaken. Numerous other changes which also occurred during the same era only catalysed this process of disenchantment from the age-old Christian worldview. Historians recognise three types of changes, viz., political, economic and intellectual changes, but by far the most important reason for the decline of this worldview was the series of intellectual changes which crystallized around 14-15th century[12].

In fact, questioning of some of the practices of church had begun even earlier with revival of learning, especially after rediscovery of Aristotelian works in the twelfth century. Aristotelian dialectic especially fascinated medieval thinkers and motivated people to question the doctrines of church. One of the earliest thinkers was Peter Abelard (1079-1142) who in his little book *Sic et non* (translated 'Yes and No') set down one hundred and fifty-eight propositions through some of which he brought out contradictory nature of the doctrines of church. He tried to advocate supremacy of reason over faith: "A doctrine is believed, not because God has said it, but because we are convinced by reason that it is so"[13]. This 'irreverence' created a stir in the church which responded by trying Abelard for insolence, but Abelard died before his case was finally heard by the Pope. Nevertheless, the methods of reasoning which Abelard advocated became quite popular and the church had to reconcile its teachings with Aristotelian dialectic. The most successful of these attempts was that of St. Thomas Aquinas who gave arguments to answer many of the questions men had been raising since the days of Abelard. In his famous work, *Summa Theologica*, he followed the dialectic method to arrive at conclusions by logical reasoning. He recognised two sources of knowledge: "the mysteries of the Christian faith as transmitted through the channel of the Scripture, of the Fathers and of Christian tradition, and the truths of human reason...of which the chief exponents were Plato and Aristotle. The two sources cannot be opposed, since they both flow from God as the one source. Hence philosophy and theology must be compatible, and a Summa Theologica should contain the whole of knowledge"(14). Even the existence of God was established by five ways of reasoning using the principle of causality!

The church was thus able to satisfy most of its critics, but in the long run this fusion of Aristotelian thought with theology did incalculable harm. By integrating premises from Christian dogma with Aristotelian philosophy, St. Thomas evolved a monolith of knowledge, the parts of which were believed to be interdependent, "so that an attack on Aristotelian philosophy or science became an attack on the Christian faith"(14). This was probably the single most important reason for Church's conflict with post-Renaissance developments in science which ultimately resulted in complete overthrowing of the Christian Worldview.

The Development of Science: Science-Religion Conflict

To any reader, who is born and brought up in the modern times, it may seem quite strange that developments in science should in any way influence the camp of religion, for we are all tuned to a world-view which sees science and religion as two distinct activities having no relationship with each other. However, if we put ourselves in the environs of that crucial transition period of 13th-15th century, the picture changes entirely. Though the church had lost much of its secular powers and also some of its grandeur and lustre, yet it continued to exert a strong influence on the Western world. Before Renaissance, all intellectual activity had been confined entirely to the church. Throughout the Middle Ages, the most coveted position for which any bright young man could aspire was that of a Father in the Church and once he reached it, all his intellectual prowess was utilised only in justifying the Christian theology. The spirit of free enquiry blossomed only after the advent of Renaissance and there was a spurt of intellectual activity, mostly outside the church.

The earliest 'scientific' work which is usually hailed as the harbinger of the spirit of free enquiry, was the book *De Revolutionibus Orbium Celestium* by Polish astronomer Nicolaus Copernicus published just a few days before his death in 1543. In this book, Copernicus proposed a helio-centric theory of cosmos (i.e., stationary sun with other planets, including earth revolving around it) in contrast to the geo-centric theory of Ptolemy (i.e., stationary earth at the centre and other heavenly bodies including sun, revolving around it) which was the 'official' theory believed by the church. The church was already stung by the loss of its secular powers to the kings and the cleavage in the church as a result of Protestant Reformation. Acceptance of helio-centric view meant repudiation of Aristotle, whose works formed the base of the giant monolith of knowledge so laboriously constructed by the schoolmen led by Aquinas. The essence of spirituality having been left long ago, the Aristotelian science, with its 'divine' explanations for all sorts of phenomena ranging from motion of heavenly bodies to human physiology, provided respectable and awe-inspiring crutch for the church. In the eyes of the church, these 'divine explanations' probably gave some sort of justification to the continued existence of its huge organisation, for it was the sole arbiter of divinity on earth. Consequently, an attack on Aristotelian 'science' (he believed in geocentric view of cosmos) was interpreted as a covert attack on the church itself, which had to be put down with a heavy hand. Accordingly Copernician theory was pronounced "false and altogether opposed to Holy Scripture"[(15)]. The institution of Holy Roman and Universal Inquisition created by Pope Paul III in 1542 to stem the spread of Reformation doctrines, was given powers (in 1571) to judge written documents and prepare a list of prohibited books, and Copernician theory soon found a place in the list. Teaching such books and even holding such beliefs was enough to warrant Inquisition, as it happened in the case of Galileo who was tried in 1633, imprisoned till he agreed to recant and then confined for the rest of life in his villa under strict house arrest. Galileo, however, was more fortunate than outspoken Giardo Bruno, who in 1600 was burnt at stake. This marked the beginning of a series of confrontations between the church and the protagonists of free enquiry (the scientists) in the modern age. In each of these, the church was finally proved wrong and had to make undignified retreat from its position. The heliocentric view was finally accepted by the church in 1822 and Darwin's theory of evolution in late twentieth century. As a result, the intellectual authority of the religious thinkers was completely destroyed within a few generations, sounding the death-knell of the Christian worldview.

The Mechanical Philosophy

The development of science in the 16th-17th century not only accelerated the extinction of the old worldview but it also gave birth to a new worldview. The doors to this new paradigm were opened by Francis Bacon who published his ideas in his classic book *Novum Orgamum* in 1620. The main emphasis of Bacon was on carrying out experiments to unravel the connections between phenomena and arrive at general laws describing nature so that the real purpose of science, viz., endowing human life with new powers and discoveries could be achieved. He derided the collected works of ancient Greeks (Plato, Aristotle and even Homer) as nothing but "*contentious learning*" for they had not "adduced a single experiment which tends to relieve and benefit the condition of man"[(16)]. *Knowledge was thus not a virtue in itself as ancient Greeks would like us to believe*[(17)] *but it was useful only if it produced some effects on our material well being.* 'Know thyself' was replaced by 'know nature' though the purpose of both these enquiries in the vision of their originators was apparently the same, viz., to be happy. Torturing secrets out of nature in order to subdue and control it, was one of the prime objects of scientific enquiry in the Baconian scheme of thinking, and therefore he stressed that rather than asking the metaphysical 'why' of things, science of learning should be committed to the 'how' of things.

It was Renes Descartes (1596–1650), famous French philosopher and mathematician (inventor of cartesian coordinate geometry) who systematically initiated the task of explaining the 'how' of numerous phenomena already known by seventeenth century. Of course, he did not do it in the Baconian way for he himself performed no experiments to uncover the 'truths'. He confined himself to evolving 'proper' interpretation of the phenomena, and in the process he originated a completely new mode of thinking what has come to be known as the Mechanical Philosophy. Basic to this mechanical philosophy is the Cartesian Dualism. "All of reality, he argued, is composed of two substances. What we may call spirit is a substance characterized by the act of thinking; the material realm is a substance the essence of which is extension. Res cogitans and res extensa–Descartes defined them in a way to distinguish and separate them absolutely. To thinking substance one cannot attribute any property characteristic of matter–not extension, not place, not motion. Thinking, which includes the various modes which mental activity assumes, and thinking alone, is its property. From the point of view of natural science, the more important result of the dichotomy lay in the rigid exclusion of any and all psychic characteristics from material nature"[(18)]. To Descartes, matter was thus really dead and possessed no activity except motion derived from God in the beginning. The Cartesian Dualism—viz. removal of every trace of psychic from the material nature—was admirably suited for the purposes of modern science and held its sway till late twentieth century when developments in quantum mechanics re-opened this question of mind-matter interaction, as we shall study later.

As its fundamental proposition, the mechanical philosophy asserted that all *phenomena of nature are produced by inert matter in motion.* Light, gravitation, magnetism and even human physiology were sought to be explained similarly by contriving some causal mechanisms[(19)]. Earlier philosophies had seen nature in organic terms. Descartes turned the tables by picturing even organic phenomena as mechanisms. Man was, of course, an exception—for he had both soul and body. But even in this case, the soul was not considered to be the seat of life, and all organic functions were described in purely mechanistic terms[20]. In fact, in his *Traite' de l'homme* (Treatise on a Man) he described a machine that performs all physiological functions of a man—circulation, digestion, nourishment, growth and perception.

A very significant consequence of the mechanical philosophy was the subordination of qualitative properties of matter. Descartes agreed with Galileo's distinction between the primary or inseparable qualities of bodies (chief amongst them being extension), and the secondary qualities like colour, taste, smell etc. As the bodies comprised only of particles of matter in motion, all the secondary qualities are merely sensations excited by bodies in motion impinging on nerves. All nature was thus converted into simple matter in motion and Descartes confidently proclaimed, "Give me extension and motion, and I will construct the Universe"[21]. The whole world was thus thought to be a giant machine, composed entirely of inert chunks of matter moving by physical necessity totally indifferent to the existence of thinking beings.

The attempts of Descartes and other mechanical philosophers to show that for all known phenomena causal mechanisms can be imagined, resulted in incorporation of some rather strange mechanisms in Descarte's Universe, and many of his contemporaries were sceptical of these attempts. Robert Boyle, the famous English chemist and philosopher, for example, did attempt to explain that everything could not be reduced to simple mathematical terms. While agreeing with the view that 'secondary qualities' are only phantoms of the sensations, he also pointed out that since man with his senses is a part of the Universe, in a sense, the secondary qualities are as real as the primary. The mechanical world and the thinking world are both parts of the whole world which philosophy has to face. It may be necessary to treat them as entirely separate from each other in order to bring the problem within human understanding; but the separation is due to our need of simplifying the problem by treating it successively from different aspects[22]. This has nothing to do with the nature of the real world as such.

But it was the Cartesian view which gained widespread acceptance, probably because people like Boyle expressed their philosophy in religious terms and the camp of religion was by then in great disfavour. Thus, by the time Descartes died in 1650, his mathematical view of nature had become acceptable to the best minds all over Europe, in spite of many weird mechanical explanations contrived by him to explain various phenomena. And slowly, with further progress of science as the explanations became more convincing, the mechanical philosophy got more and more deeply entrenched.

The greatest contribution in this direction was probably made by Newton who, by introducing the concept of force, to already existing notions of matter and motion, reconciled mathematical mechanics to the mechanical philosophy. Strictly speaking, the concept of gravitational force was not in harmony with the prevailing philosophy, for Newton gave no 'mechanism' to explain its origin, and he was often criticised for being 'unscientific' and trying to reintroduce 'occult quantities'. In the end, Newton did acknowledge this criticism to an extent in the second edition of *Optiks* in 1717, wherein he tried to explain the action of gravity by means of an aether pervading the Universe—such was the strong compulsion of the mechanical philosophy!

Nevertheless, the compromise was only apparent for Newtonian aether was composed of particles which repelled each other at a distance[23]. Newton considered the forces between particles as ontological realities, and was humble enough to admit that he did not know their final cause–in fact, he referred them directly to the agency of God. He likened himself to a child finding petty pebbles on the shore while the ocean of truth lay unknown before him.

But others — especially his French followers—were less cautious. They believed that the Newtonian system only validated the Cartesian vision of reality as a great machine. Newton's and Descartes' references to God were soon overlooked as unnecessary and overshadowed by the achievements of their mathematical mechanics. Newton had invoked the benevolence of God to periodically set the solar system in order after it had got deranged, either due to external causes (falling comets etc.) or due to its innate nature. Once Laplace proved that the perturbations produced either by mutual influences or by external bodies such as comets were only temporary, and that the Solar System was inherently stable, this was seen as further 'proof' of redundancy of the concept of God[24]. All this led to the revival of philosophy of materialism—a belief that hard matter in unyielding lumps is the sole ultimate reality of the Universe.

Revival of Materialism

Numerous developments in other fields of science only further strengthened this belief. Thus, Lavoiser's experiments with combustion of mercury not only demystified 'fire' but also established that in spite of all apparent changes, matter is conserved even after chemical action. This was seen to remove one of the fundamental objections to the 'reality' of matter, viz., its evanescent nature, its 'apparent' decay and change which had been the most prominent reason advanced by philosophers of antiquity, like Plato, to deny the reality of matter, and thence that of the world of sense. Matter does not really decay or 'die'; it is only transformed by recombinations such was the clear message of Lavoiser's experiments, and quite naturally it strengthened the view that matter was an ultimate reality.

Thus, by the beginning of eighteenth century most of the known physical phenomena could be explained on the basis of mechanical philosophy. However, in spite of Descartes', attempts, living organisms and especially human beings still remained an enigma. The developments in the eighteenth and nineteenth century gradually brought these also within the fold of the philosophy of materialism. Thus, the applicability of the principle of conservation of energy to the living organism seemed to blur the distinction between a 'heat engine' and a living being. It was now seen that animals (human beings included), like machines, can only move and do work when supplied with energy from without—with fuel in the form of food and with air containing oxygen. The theory of vitalism, which held that in living beings there exists a vital force (something not material) which regulates its proper functioning, thus received a severe jolt, or at least so thought the philosophers. The synthetic preparation of a number of organic substances which make up living matter further diluted the belief in spiritual interpretation of life as it had been previously thought that complicated substances, characteristic of animal and vegetable tissues, could only be formed by 'vital process.' The belief arose that physiology was but a special case of "the physics of colloids and the chemistry of proteids," and that it should be possible to explain all the activities—physical, biological and even psychological—of the living organisms as mere modes of motion of molecules and manifestations of mechanical or chemical energy. The most lethal blow on the bastion of 'spirituality' was probably made by Darwin's Theory of Evolution, by explaining the origin of all species on the basis of the concepts of chance variation—now known as random mutation and natural selection. There was no need to invoke the agency of God as a creator of human beings or of any other species, and the old argument for theism based on the presence of design in the organic world was exploded. Even Man—whom theology had hitherto projected as the supreme creation of God—had evolved as a result of chance variations from 'lower' species (probably apes). Later Drawinians, of whom Haeckel in Germany was the most prominent, extended this evolution to embrace both organic and inorganic nature, and argued (without any evidence!) that the simplest form of living protoplasm arose from non-living nitrogenous carbon compounds by a process of spontaneous generation. Like the magnetic property of the ferrous group of elements and the radioactive property of the radioactive group of elements, it was thus believed that Life was essentially a property of the carbon atoms. Even consciousness and thinking were sought to be explained on purely materialistic basis as arising from the "functions of the ganglionic cells of the cortex of the brain"[(25)]. All the fields of science thus seemed to echo in unison, '*matter is the sole reality*.' The philosophy of materialism was thus deeply entrenched in majority of the men of science.

From Materialism to Materialistic Worldview

From a purely philosophic point of view, there is not much difference between a materialistic worldview and the philosophy of materialism, for, if matter is the sole reality, and the human beings just a result of fortuitous combination of some atoms, there can be no other purpose of human life than seeking enjoyment through material interaction. However, historically the materialistic worldview did not develop through such philosophic argumentation but as a result of application of the mechanical philosophy to sciences dealing essentially with human and social institutions.

One of the earliest systematic attempts of this kind was made by John Locke in late seventeenth century who believed that the chaos in the society was the result of its being based on irrational tradition and custom that originated from theocentrism. He set for himself the task of discovering the 'natural laws' by adhering to which social order could be achieved quite akin to the 'harmony ' of mechanical systems based on Newtonian mechanics. Starting in this manner, like a Cartesian philosopher, he quickly concluded that God could not be the proper basis of Government since, by definition, God is unknowable.* In a stroke, he thus made the monumental break of advocating a dissociation of religion from public activity—something which is axiomatically assumed to be desirable even in modern age. The result of this monumental break is best put in the words of Jeremy Rifkin[26]: "Having removed God from the affairs of people—as Bacon had removed Him from nature—Locke was left with human beings all alone in the universe... Now, men and women became just what Bacon, Descartes and Newton had made of nature: mere physical phenomena interacting

---

*Since knowledge, in cartesian paradigm, could consist only of systematised sensory information.

with other bits of matter in the cold, mechanical universe. This being the case, on what basis could a social order be formed?... Once we cut through useless custom and superstition, argued Locke, we see that society, being made up solely of individuals creating their own meaning, has one purpose only: to protect and allow for the increase of the property of its members. Pure self-interest thus becomes the sole basis for the establishment of the state,... for reason leads us to conclude that this is the natural order of things...." The result of this philosophy is quite obvious. "Society properly becomes materialistic... each individual is called upon to act out his role of social atom...attempting to amass personal wealth." The contrast from the medieval Goal of "seeking salvation and not achieving things" could not be more glaring. In its place was the new idea of seeking perfection in this world. The idea of progress was thus born. History was henceforth to be seen as progressive journey from rather disordered and confused state that society found itself in, to the predictable well-ordered state symbolised by the Newtonian world machine.

Adam Smith carried forward these ideas of Locke in formulating a theory of economics and concluded that the most efficient method of economic organization is *laissez-faire* the general principle of non-interference with the free action of the individual. Like Locke, Smith also recognised selfishness as something 'natural' and did not like the idea of erecting social and moral barriers to its pursuit, and instead believed that there was an 'invisible hand' of 'Providence' which governed the economic processes so as to "make nearly the same distribution of the necessaries of life which would have been made had the earth been divided into equal proportions among all its inhabitants"[27]. Unfortunately, this 'invisible hand' of 'Providence' did not really operate the way Smith had theorized and his policy of *laissez-faire* only promoted the quest for material abundance to satisfy physical needs, without paying any heed to ethics. This side stepping of ethics in fact became the hallmark of all later mainstream economists resulting in a belief that what is 'pleasant' is 'good' and what is 'unpleasant' is evil.

Human being came to be recognized as a 'felicity computer' under the sway of the forces of pleasure and pain—quite akin to a physical body whose movement through space reflects the forces of attraction and repulsion, governed by Newtonian mechanics. The whole philosophy of utilitarianism, first formulated by an Englishman Jeremy Bentham originated from such concepts, and is succinctly summed up in Bentham's famous phrase: "Nature has placed mankind under the governance of two sovereign masters, pain and pleasure. It is for them *alone* to point out what we ought to do, as well as to determine what we should do."[(28)] The implication of Bentham's assertion is clear. Men should act in a manner that maximizes his 'pleasure' and minimizes the 'pain'. The contrast from the medieval worldview which advocated equanimity in the face of sensory interactions could not be more glaring. By thus reducing all those perennial questions of 'right' and 'wrong', the true basis of wisdom etc. to the matter of 'pleasure' and 'pain', a theoretical framework was prepared justifying the materialistic worldview.

This theoretical framework was further strengthened at the 'micro' level when psychologists modelled their study of human behaviour after the mechanical philosophy. Two streams of psychologists emerged. The behaviourists who saw living organisms as machines that react to external stimuli, and the psychoanalysts (led by Freud) who propounded that human behaviour was essentially controlled by the unconscious desires and impulses stored deep inside human psyche. Both the schools thus agreed that human beings are basically automata; while behaviourists said that the 'response' of these automata was governed essentially by external stimuli, psychoanalysts believed it to be governed by the 'unconscious mind.' The obvious implication of this mechanistic psychology is that we can neither build our characters nor mould our lives and since we are powerless to control the future, we may as well make the best of life as it is and take what comes to us without striving to have it different. The Epicurean doctrine of 'let us eat and drink, for tomorrow we die' is thus clearly advocated resulting in contemptuous abandonment of those inhibitions and restraints conventionally termed as morals. In fact the school of psychoanalysts related neurotic disorders to suppression of deep-seated desires due to compulsions of morality. Crass materialism could not ask for more respectable scientific footing! And when Darwin's Theory of Evolution was interpreted by social philosophers like Herbert Spencer to sanctify the philosophy of 'survival of fittest' as the Law of Nature, the journey of modern civilization to the pinnacle of materialistic worldview was nearly complete. With survival at the expense of others recognised as the main aim of life, the values hitherto considered as undesirable such as arrogance and ruthlessness came to be regarded as virtues (since they help in survival). Only thus can one account for what Lord Keynes said in 1930: "For at least another hundred years we must pretend to ourselves and to everyone that fair is foul and foul is fair; for foul is useful and fair is not. Avarice and usury and precaution must be our Gods for a little longer still. For only they can lead us out of the tunnel of economic necessity into daylight"[(30)]. The most candid enunciation of this worldview, which brings out its contrast with the medieval 'Christian worldview' mentioned earlier, was done by Nietzsche[(29)]. Firmly convinced that it was the 'moralic acid' which was eating into the race and infecting it with disease like sympathy and pity, he suggested means to improve the race. It is a well known fact that "those who are sick and degenerate should not communicate their illness and degeneracy to those that are healthy", and therefore, he argued cogently, it was in the interest of a higher race that "the weak and botched should perish and should even be helped to perish"[(29)]. Only then could a race of 'supermen' (Ubermensch) emerge whose 'virtues' would be exuberance of life, ruthless egoism, arrogance, revenge against people, hate and anger—the morals of the masters. Many historians believe that it was this philosophy which was sought to be implemented by Nazis during the Second World War, which should in fact be viewed as a 'natural' outcome of the materialistic worldview, as we shall see in detail in the next chapter.

NOTES

1. Historians usually divide various periods of antiquity as

   Ancient Greek–Earlier to 4 Century B.C.

Hellenistic Era		323 BC to 31 BC
Roman Age		32 BC to 476 AD
Middle Ages	Early	476 AD (fall of Roman empire)– 1000 AD
	Late	1000 AD – 1500 AD
Modern Period		Sixteenth Century onwards

2. Mumford, Lewis, *The Myth of the Machine–Technics and Human Development*, Harcourt, Brace and World Inc., NY. 1966; p 257-8.
3. Some of the more famous dialogues of Plato are Criton, Apology, Phaedo, The Republic, Timmeaus.
4. Windelband, W., *A History of Philosophy,* The Macmillan Co., NY, 1901; p. 82.
5. Quotation from Plato's *Republic* has been taken from its abridged version given by Kaplan, J.D., "Dialogues of Plato", Washington Square Press, 1951; p. 361.
6. Sarton, G. : A History of Science–Ancient Science through the Golden Age of Greece, *Science Editions*, John Wiley and Sons, Inc., NY, 1952; p. 398.
7. Quotations from New Testament have been adopted from 'SHRI KHRIST GITA'–*compiled by D. Fakirbhai, Unity Books; ISPCK, Delhi, 1969.*
8. Ibid, p28,40
9. Ellul, Jacques; *The Technological Society*, Jonathan Cape, London, 1965, p 37. A powerful critique of modern technological society.
10. Rogers, A.K., *A Student's History of Philosophy*, Macmillan, NY, Third Ed., 1935, p. 190.
11. Magofin, R.V.D. and Duncalf, F. *Ancient and Medieval History*, Silver Burdett Co., NJ, 1959; p. 694.
12. Ibid. p. 782-784.
13. Ibid. p. 608.
14. Dampier, W.C., *A History of Science*, Cambridge Univ. Press, 1961; p. 86.
15. Ibid. p. 113.

16. Rifkin, J. and T Howard, *Entropy – A new worldview*, Viking Press, NY, 1980, p. 19.

17. The contrast between ancient and modern points of view is brought out by the following anecdote. Euclid, on being asked by a pupil at the end of his first lesson in Geometry what he would get by learning such things, is said to have called his servant and remarked, "Give him a coin since he must... make gain by what he learns".

18. Westfall, R.S., *The Construction of Modern Science: Mechanisms and Mechanics*, John Wiley and Sons., N.Y., 1971, p. 31.

19. The above reference gives in simple terms some details of the mechanisms–often weird–devised by Descartes to explain Gravitation, Light etc. Some extracts: 'Thus Descartes' universe was a plenum. The equation of matter with extension meant that every extended space must, by definition, be filled with matter–or better, must be matter. There can be no vacuum. If there is no empty space into which a body can move, how is it possible that there be any motion at all? It is possible, Descartes replied, only because every body that moves, moves into the space that it vacates, as it were, at the same time. Put in other terms, every moving particle in a plenum must participate in a closed circuit of moving matter, like the rim of a wheel turning on its axis. Hence every motion must be circular...i.e., in a close orbit of some shape." Descartes explained major phenomena of nature as the consequence of the centrifugal pressures arising from this circular motion. Thus light was explained as a consequence of centrifugal pressures arising from the vortex of solar system centred around sun. The sensation called 'light' was essentially the motion induced in optic nerve due to this pressure acting on the retina of the eye.

    Similar vortical theories were devised to explain gravitation and magnetism. See Westfall, op.cit., p. 36-37.

20. Thus, the heart became a tea kettle, its heat analogous to the heat of fermentation (in itself a mechanical process according to Descartes), its action, the boiling and expansion of the drops of blood which were forced into it from the veins and forced out by the pressure of vaporization. Other animals, lacking a rational soul, were nothing but complicated machines. If there were automata, Descartes asserted, "...possessing the organs and outward form of a monkey or some other animal without reason, we should not have had any means of ascertaining that they were not of the same nature as those animals".

    Westfall, op.cit., p. 38.

21. Randall, J.H., *The Making of the Modern Mind*, Cambridge Mass, Houghton, Mifflin, 1940, p. 259.

22. Dampier, W.C., op.cit., p. 139.

23. Westfall, R.S., op.cit., p. 157.

24. It is mentioned by historians that when Laplace went to present his compendium *Mecanique Celeste* to Emperor Napoleon, the Emperor remarked: "M. Laplace, they tell me you have written this large book on the system of the universe, and have never even mentioned its Creator." To this remark, Laplace answered bluntly, "Je n'ai pas besoin de cette hypothese"'. (There was no need of such a hypothesis).

    Edwards Paul (Editor in Chief), *The Encyclopaedia of Philosophy*, Vol. III, Macmillan Co. and the Free Press, NY, 1967, p. 399.

26. Rifkin, J., op.cit, p. 24-25.

27. Lutz, M.A. and K. Lux, *The Challenge of Humanistic Economics*, The Benjamin Cummins Publishing Co. Inc., California, 1979, p. 28.

28. Bentham, J, quoted in ibid. p. 6.

29. Rogers A. K., op.cit., p 469-470.

30. Lord Keynes, quoted in Schumacher, E.F., "Small is Beautiful," Abacus Press 1974, p. 19.

4 MODERN PREDICAMENT AND THE MATERIALISTIC WORLD VIEW

The deer, the elephant, the moth, the fish and the black bee—these five are killed through their own attachment, being tied to only one of the five senses, viz., sound etc. What then is in store for man who is attached to all these five (senses)?

Adi Sankaracharaya
Vivekchudamani, Verse 76

The preceeding chapters clearly hint that the predicament in which modern civilization finds itself is largely an outcome of the materialistic paradigm which it has so enthusiastically embraced over last four centuries. And now this very embrace seems to be throttling the mankind. Unfortunately the squeeze is so gentle that we are unable to discern it. In fact, we even seem to 'enjoy' it—quite like a frog who would jump unceasingly if put on a hot pan but would allow itself to be 'deep fried' in a milder fire. Thus, we find a large section of people giving a tacit acceptance to the maladies of modern civilization as the inevitable 'price of progress', so much so that even colossal tragedies like the industrial genocide at Bhopal do not stir the dormant humanity out of its slumber. When confronted with such serious maladies—which are often sought to be projected as 'accidents' or 'aberrations'—all types of immediate causes are 'identified' and numerous solutions and remedial measures—scientific, technological, social, political, economic and even religious — are suggested, but rarely would people question the desirability of the race for material 'progress' which is at the root of these maladies. The grip of materialistic worldview is so strong that we are unable to get out of its groove and dispassionately analyze various maladies and isolate their root cause. It therefore becomes extremely important that we try to understand the full implications of the materialistic worldview so as to create an awareness of the dangers inherent in it and thus initiate the search for an alternate paradigm.

Materialism and Strife

To understand clearly the connection between materialistic worldview and the increasing strife at all levels, viz., individual, societal, national and international, which is the prime malady of modern civilization, let us restate the basic tenet of this paradigm. A materialist believes that to increase his happiness he must increase the 'goods' and 'services' at his disposal.

Now, this obviously demands skill and capability of a certain kind which will certainly not be present to equal degree in all the members of any society. Consequently, some are bound to have more and others less of these artefacts of happy living. The society thus gets stratified into 'haves' and 'have-nots'. The materialistic paradigm forces both these strata to keep on increasing their levels of consumption, for only thus can they increase their happiness which is the basic urge of every human being. It is quite natural that by the very fact of their being 'haves', this section of society will be able to increase the quantum of 'goods' at their disposal at a much faster rate than the 'have-nots' and thus the gap between them will be ever widening. Clearly, the natural outcome of this ever-widening gap would be jealousy which ultimately breeds ill-will and hatred. The groove of materialistic worldview forces the 'have-nots' to believe that the 'haves' are Shylocks prospering at their cost while the 'haves' believe that the 'have-nots' are foolish, lazy, good-for-nothing people who rightly suffer. The ill-will and hatred thus get logical support and are deeply entrenched. The result: even at the slightest pretext these manifest their true form, viz., violence. This, in fact, is the root, of majority of strife in the free society today, be it at the individual level (like petty crimes, thefts, robberies), at a community level (terrorism, riots) or even at national level (political instability, civil wars, international wars etc.).

The above arguments are often countered by the historical 'evidence' of the middle ages, when the western society was full of strife, though the worldview was not materialistic. Violence is thus sought to be projected as an inalienable part of human society which persists whatever be the worldview. A careful analysis, however, reveals that this is not really so. One of the main causes of strife in western Europe during the Middle Ages was again the tremendous gap between the impoverished barbarians and the wealthy empires they ultimately ravaged. Slowly, as these barbarians became 'kings' they sought to perpetuate their power and status by invading the less mighty chieftains, and therefore Europe was full of fighting, especially during later period of Middle Ages. These barbarians were certainly not the embodiments of the 'Christian worldview'. And as far as the 'religious' wars are concerned, as discussed earlier in Chapter 3, these were the result of inadequate understanding of the essence of spirituality due to slow degeneration in the camp of religion.

There is of course another dimension of this debate which cannot be overlooked, viz., the tremendous difference between the degree of violence which modern civilization is capable of and that which has ever happened in the recorded history of mankind. The potency of the agents of destruction which have been created in last fifty years staggers imagination. It is estimated that the two super-powers have enough nuclear warheads with them which can destroy the whole humanity many times over[(1)]. And, as if that was not enough, should there be any freak survivors of a nuclear war, the planet earth would no longer be fit for their habitation.

Since stratification in the society is the immediate cause of strife, it often appears that by reducing the gap between the rich and the poor through 'proper' wage structure and legislative measures, the strife could be eliminated. But again, this is also a superficial way of attacking the problem since the root, viz., the materialistic paradigm remains intact. When its natural manifestation in the form of disparity in the society is suppressed (through whatever means, be it taxation or wage control), it shows itself in another form, viz., increased tensions at the individual level. This arises from the fact that to reduce disparity while retaining the materialistic paradigm demands tremendous stifling of freedom — freedom to speak, to trade, and even freedom to gather knowledge—through strict legislative means which is bound to result in increased tension due to a feeling of suffocation, fear, and even loss of self-esteem. And a society composed of people living in 'fear' with a constant feeling of suffocation cannot remain stable for long!*

The message seems quite clear if only we are willing to see the writing on the wall—we have to abandon the materialistic paradigm if we wish to eradicate ever increasing internecine conflicts.

Materialism and Ecology

If increasing strife is leading modern civilization to self-destruction, the grave ecological imbalances are threatening its very existence on this planet. And, as has been brought out in Chapter 2, modern technology which is deeply anchored in the materialistic paradigm is at the root of this impending disaster. When 'wants' become 'needs', the natural outcome is wanton exploitation of available resources. One doesn't need to be a genius to see the likely consequences of this paradigm. Clearly, there would be a rapid depletion of the earth's resources and a degradation of the environment. The former follows from the simple fact that we are living on a finite-sized planet with finite reserves of fossil fuels and minerals. The degradation of the environment follows from

---

* The recent fall of communist regimes in Eastern Europe and the disintegration of Soviet Union validate these arguments.

the paradigm itself, for it costs lesser to dump toxic wastes into rivers or atmosphere than to process these to reduce their harmful effects. And as well documented studies show[2], we have already reached a stage where most of our mineral resources and fossil fuels (except, probably coal) would be extinct in another 50 years, if we continue to cater to the spiralling demands for 'goods' and 'services'. A society entirely dependent on these endowments of humanity, and yet eating away this capital rapaciously cannot last long—though precise estimates may differ. And considering the rate at which we are polluting our rivers and the atmosphere, we may also run out of water to drink and air to breathe!

Certainly it is not a happy situation unless we refuse to accept the right of existence of our grandchildren.

Materialism and Dehumanisation

A subtle and therefore more potent effect of materialistic paradigm is the continuous dehumanization of individuals. Of course, to define exactly the term 'dehumanization' demands a clear understanding of what it means to be a human being—which alas is lacking even now in modern scientific civilization! Here, by the term dehumanization, we mean a degeneration in all those endeavours which distinguish human beings from rest of the species, e.g., craftsmanship, art, poetry, literature, dramatics, music, sports, education, politics, marriage and family life, fellow-feeling and compassion etc. A dispassionate analysis reveals that in each of these truly human endeavours the materialistic paradigm has brought about a noticeable degeneration thus reducing human beings to the level of animals. The materialistic paradigm with its sweeping emphasis on cost-benefit analysis for all decision making, and the philosophy of reductionism (which is one of the foundation stones of the philosophy of materialism) have created such a groove in the minds of masses that they now find it difficult to discern beauty in art, literature and even music. Charles Darwin's testimony to this effect is most revealing[3].

"Upto the age of thirty, or beyond it, poetry of many kinds gave me great pleasure, and even as a school boy I took intense delight in Shakespeare, especially in the historical plays...formerly pictures gave me considerable, and music very great delight. But now for many years I cannot endure to read a line of poetry: I have tried lately to read Shakespeare, and found it so intolerably dull that it nauseated me. I have also lost almost any taste for pictures or music... My mind seems to have become a kind of machine for grinding general laws out of large collections of fact, but why this should have caused the atrophy of that part of the brain alone, on which the higher tastes depend, I cannot conceive... The loss of these tastes is a loss of happiness, and may possibly be injurious to the intellect, and more probably to the moral character, by enfeebling the emotional part of our nature."

As is clear from Darwin's words, this 'enfeebling' of the emotional part of our nature is a direct outcome of our attitude of giving importance only to quantifiable phenomena and excluding them from other non-quantifiable phenomena with which they may be naturally connected. And, as has been pointed out by Skolimowski(4), this continual practice of 'conceptual alienation' which forms the bedrock of modern science (and hence modern civilization), paves the way for 'psychological alienation' which is at the root of increasing alienation in social and human relations. The result: increasing privitization which is only abetted by modern technological innovations like radio, TV and video. This loss of tastes, and privitization of life reflects in the decline in public participation in any community activity, be it dramatics, poetry recitation or folk dances, community singing or music or even election meetings. Man no longer seems to be even a social animal!

The degeneration in the field of sports is probably the most direct pointer to deep influence of materialism. An activity which was meant to be an ideal combine of entertainment, healthcare and community participation, an opportunity to learn basic human values of cooperation, forbearance and brotherhood has been reduced, in majority of the cases, to a lucrative business for the players as well as the organisers. The traditional bonhomie seems to have been left far behind and replaced by animosity and cut-throat competition, so much so that the modern 'sportsmen' do not hesitate to use any means — ranging from drugs to bribery—to win the coveted prizes. 'Sportsmanspirit' does not any longer belong to the sports!

The degradation in the field of education due to the prevailing materialistic paradigm is probably most evident in our own country. For both students as well as parents, the main objective of education today is to 'earn' a 'degree' which would enable them to secure a good job with a fat salary and heavy 'perks'. Even well-meaning intellectuals seem to give consent to this truncated concept of education as a prelude to vocational training. The best education, we are now told, is that which enables its recipients to become job creators rather than job seekers; that's why we find such a craze for 'professional' education. Everybody wishes to become an engineer or a doctor or an accountant or a manager etc. The schools and universities are no longer the seats of wisdom and enlightenment but only 'living' extensions of hospitals and factories where their products would ultimately fit in. Is there any thing to wonder then if today we see rampant corruption and moral degradation? As the young children are educated only to maximise their earnings should we not feel proud if they devise ingenious means (like smuggling, hoarding, accepting bribes, extortion etc.) to achieve this objective? The invasion of materialistic worldview in the domain of education is clearly sowing the seeds of anarchy.

Probably the most blatant dehumanizing aspect of modern materialistic culture reveals itself in transformation of the 'sacred' institution of marriage into a business deal which is so evident today both in the east and the west. In our own country it manifests in the form of demands for dowry at the marriage, (leading many a time even to 'bride burning') as a quick means of acquiring 'riches'. And in the west it is manifesting in the form of tremendous spurt in the divorce rate. From the pristine concept of holy matrimony where the partners vowed and prayed 'till death do us part', the modern materialistic view of marriage is a great contrast. Says Becker[5] in his celebrated work *A Theory of Marriage* : "Each marriage can be considered a two-person firm with either member being the 'entrepreneur' who 'hires' the other at...a salary...and receives residual 'profits'...." With such a crass materialistic conception of marriage is it any wonder that these 'two-person firms' called families are disintegrating at a fast pace for dissolution of such 'firms' and regrouping of partners might be the best economic strategy?[6] And with disintegration of family, which is the basic building block of any organised society, the very survival is at stake.

Concluding Remarks

The above discussion makes it pretty clear that at the root of most of the serious maladies of modern times—be it the ecological crisis, or increasing violence or social maladies like corruption or disintegration of family life lies the materialistic worldview which we seem to have embraced so fondly. Unlike the problems with which any civilization has been beset in the past, these are of a nature which threaten the very survival of human race and the suitability of this planet to retain life. It therefore seems imperative that an all-out effort be made to shed off this materialistic paradigm for it has failed miserably in giving peace and happiness to mankind. What the alternative can be is thus the immediate question.

Fortunately, there have been sincere attempts at answering this question by resurrecting the ancient wisdom which holds the key to the alternate paradigm that could usher an era of permanent peace and happiness. Swami Vivekananda, Swami Ramatirtha and numerous other saints following them have heralded, early in the twentieth century, *a new Renaissance–the Renaissance of spirituality* which opens the doors to a scientific understanding of the true purpose of human life and of various paths available to achieve it. Only such an understanding can be the true basis of human wlfare, as we shall discuss in detail in Chapter 6.

The materialistic worldview has also been lately questioned in the scientific community itself, which as we saw in Chapter 3, was largely responsible for the dethronement of the Christian Worldview in the sixteenth/seventeenth century. The latest discoveries in the field of Relativity and Quantum Mechanics have seriously challenged the Newtonian mechanistic picture of the physical world. The fundamental concepts of reductionism and objectivity of matter are being thrown overboard with the result that the mechanical philosophy, which is rooted in these concepts, seems to be on the verge of being rejected by its progenitors, for, as succinctly summed up sixty years ago by Whitehead.... "What is the sense of talking about a mechanical explanation when you do not know what you mean by mechanics?"

The latest discoveries in the fields of chemistry, biology and neurophysiology also confirm the trend that the classical mechanical conception of nature is seriously in error and needs to be replaced by a more holistic view which is in tune with the ancient mystical idea that the Universe is One. We shall discuss some of these interesting developments of modern science in Chapter 5.

NOTES

1. Kothari, D.S.; *Role of Science in Promoting Social and Moral Values*, V. Ramakrishna Memorial Lecture, IIT Delhi, 1983.
2. Donella H. Meadows et.al. *The Limits to Growth*, Sec. Ed. Universe Books, Potomac Associates, Washington, 1974.
3. Charles Darwin : Autobiography quoted by E.F. Schumacher "Small is Beautiful", Abacus Edition, Sphere Books, London, 1974, p.80.
4. Henryk Skolimowski, Commentary on 'Twin Moralities of Science' by S. Toulmin, p. 124 in *Science and Society, Past, Present and Future* Ed. NH Steneck, Univ. of Michigan Press, 1975.
5. Gary Becker, *A Theory of Marriage*, p. 310 quoted in *Economic Perspectives on the Family* by Isabel V. Sawhill, p. 115 in Daedalus, Spring 1977 issue *The Family*.
6. In his paper, "An Economic Analysis of Marital Instability" (in *Journal of Political Economy*, 1977, 85, 6, p 1143), Gary Becker says:

   ..."By assumption each marital 'Strategy' produces a known amount of full wealth... and the opportunity set equals the set of full wealths produced by all conceivable marital strategies. The individual ranks all strategies by their full wealth and chooses the highest. Even with certainty, a strategy with marriage, then dissolution and eventually remarriage might be preferred to all other strategies and would be anticipated at the time of first marriage. Dissolution would be a response perhaps to the growing up of children, or to the *diminishing marginal utility* from living with the same person, and would be a fully anticipated part of the variation in marital status over the life cycle".
7. Whitehead, A.N., *Science and the Modern World*, Macmillan (Mentor Books), NY, 1925, p. 23.

PART II

THE EMERGING ALTERNATIVE

5 THE PARADIGM EMERGING FROM TWENTIETH CENTURY DEVELOPMENTS IN SCIENCE

The physicist-philosopher of the twentieth century must look beyond physics to the borderland of the material and spiritual worlds. For religion has become possible for a man of science mainly because the philosophical trend of scientific thought has been startlingly redirected by the discoveries of men like Einstein, Heisenberg and Bohr in the field of relativity and quantum physics.

—Sir Arthur Eddington

The transition to twentieth century has been remarkable in more than one way. Not only did it herald a renaissance in the field of religion, (discussed in Chapter 6) but it also saw a series of revolutionary developments in the field of science which are seriously challenging the Newtonian Vision of Universe as a Giant Machine. The Quantum Theory, seeds of which were sown by Max Planck at the dawn of twentieth century (in 1900), and the Theory of Relativity, enunciated in its simplest form by Einstein in 1905, demand such an incisive departure from the 'Newtonian' and our 'common sense' view of nature that it has taken, even for the scientific community, more than fifty years to be able to appreciate the 'New paradigm' projected by these theories. And as in the post-Renaissance development of science, various other sciences (e.g. biology, medicine, neurosciences, psychology etc.) are also undergoing metamorphosis, some independently and some as a result of attempts at imbibing the new conceptual framework created by these theories of 'new physics'. There are already some signs in the horizon that the paradigm emerging from these twentieth century developments in science could eventually lead to a 'holistic' or 'humanistic' worldview which could replace the materialistic worldview with which a certain amount of disenchantment has already set in. In this chapter we shall attempt to bring out the salient features of this emerging paradigm.

Newtonian World Machine and the New Physics

To put the mind-boggling nature of New Physics in proper perspective, let us first recall the salient features of the mechanical view of Universe developed during 16–19th centuries. Its main thesis is: The whole Universe is essentially a phantasmagoria created by hard unyielding lumps of matter in motion. This movement is under the influence of a variety of forces (e.g. gravitational, electric, magnetic etc.) experienced by the matter and is governed by a few simple laws like the Newton's Laws of Motion, Conservation of Momentum etc. All the physical phenomena could thus be explained by suitably combining the laws governing motion and the laws determining the magnitude of forces between the lumps of matter.

This conception – usually termed as Newtonian world machine – thus presents a completely deterministic view of the Universe so that, in the oft quoted words of Laplace,

> "An intelligence knowing at a given instant of time all forces acting in nature as well as the momentary positions of all things of which the universe consists, would be able to comprehend the motion of the largest bodies of the world and those of the lightest atoms in one single formula, provided his intellect were sufficiently powerful to subject all data to analysis*, to him nothing would be

*A modern super-computer could probably have met these requirements of Laplace.

uncertain, *both past and future would be present to his eyes.*"[1]

Though Laplace's assertion may appear audacious to us today, his supreme confidence in the power of Newtonian paradigm was not unfounded, for these basic concepts had been applied with spectacular success to a whôle spectrum of phenomena ranging from orderly motion of giant planets to the chaotic motion of molecules in a gas. Thermal, optical, electric, magnetic—almost all phenomena known by nineteenth century fitted nicely into this mould. However, as the edifice grew upwards, sinister cracks began to appear and by the end of nineteenth century the entire structure began to crumble under the bombardment of new facts[2].

One such fundamental fact was the constancy of velocity of light irrespective of the velocity of the observer, and this defied all attempts at explanation within the classical paradigm. Thermal radiation also could not be explained satisfactorily, and finally radioactivity – spontaneous disintegration of uranium, radium and other chemical elements – was completely inexplicable by any of the models of classical physics for the atom. The Newtonian physics had clearly reached an impasse out of which it could not come out only through 'normal science'[3]. A 'paradigm shift' was called for, and this is what exactly happened with enunciation of the quantum and relativity theories.

Theory of Relativity and Newtonian Mechanics

The Theory of Relativity gives a serious jolt to some of the fundamental tenets of mechanical philosophy and Newtonian mechanics. Thus, the Newtonian (and the common-sense) conception of events occurring in absolute space over time is, according to Einstein, untenable for space and time are inseparable. In the oft quoted words of Minkowski[4], "space by itself and time by itself...are mere shadows" of a four-dimensional space-time continuum which is an 'independent reality'. Unfortunately, we can have no direct sensory experience of this four-dimensional space-time continuum and it is difficult even to describe it in ordinary language or even at the level of intuition. We can only appreciate its import through its implications at the sense-perception level. Thus, the statement 'space by itself...is a mere shadow' implies that just as it makes no sense in our everyday life to ask for the real length of somebody's shadow, similarly it makes no sense to ask for the 'real' size of an object...."The shadow is a projection of points in the three-dimensional space on to a two-dimensional plane, and its length will be different for different angles of projection. Similarly, the length of a moving object is the projection of points in four-dimensional space-time on to three-dimensional space, and its length is different in different frames of reference"[5]. Through simple mathematical transformations, Einstein established that the 'length' of an object will be reduced in the direction of motion, and this has been experimentally verified in the case of subatomic particles moving at extremely high velocities. The Cartesian (and common- sense) conception of geometric shape (*res extensa*) being an intrinsic characteristic of the objects, independent of the act of observation is thus falsified.

Even more mind-boggling is the conclusion with respect to time for, like space, this too depends on the frame of reference. It turns out that time intervals become longer, i.e., the clocks run slower as the velocity relative to the observer increases. And since these clocks could be of any type, ranging from mechanical and atomic clocks to heartbeats or brain-waves in human beings, many unbelievable conclusions emerge from this dialation of time. Thus considering the case of an astronaut who blasts off in the year 2000 and achieves a velocity of 2.6×10^8 m/s, if he returns from the space travel in A.D. 2040, he will only be 20 years older, rather than 40 years, in terms of his own bodily functions[6], because all of them would have slowed down by a factor of 2. The astronaut himself would not notice anything unusual, but if he had a twin brother staying back on earth, he would suddenly realise that his brother was now much older. This famous 'twin-brother paradox' and many other similar paradoxes which emerge from relativistic mechanics clearly shatter the conventional notion of absolute time flowing from past, through present, to future. In fact, even the terms 'past' and 'present' as used in everyday parlance lose significance since events which are 'seen' as occurring simultaneously by one observer will occur in different temporal sequence for others[7].

Probably the most important conclusion of this inseparability of space and time which cuts at the roots of classical conception of matter is the inter-convertibility of mass and energy. The mass of an object, it emerges, is like its geometric shape, no longer an 'intrinsic' property of the object but dependent 'on the velocity relative to the observer[8]. Our common-sense notion of the mass of an object, 'belonging' to the object alone, 'indifferent' to the act of observation is thus shattered. This situation is beautifully summed up by Capra[8], "In classical physics, the mass of an object had always been associated with an indestructible material substance, with some stuff of which all things were thought to be made. Relativity theory showed that mass had nothing to do with any substance, but is a form of energy. Energy however is a dynamic quantity associated with activity or with processes... a particle has (therefore) to be conceived as a dynamic pattern, a process involving the energy which manifests itself as the particle's mass." The above conclusions are borne out by the experiments on subatomic 'particles' which can be created from energy and can 'vanish' into energy. Einstein's theory of relativity thus demands a substantial change in the physicist's conception of the world, and a fundamental revision in the classical notion of objectivity. It shows that even the so-called primary qualities of objects like geometric shape (*res extensa* of Descartes) and 'mass' cannot be ascribed solely to the object irrespective of the observer for these depend upon their relative velocities. The only reason that we do not observe this dependence in usual work is that the magnitude of this relative velocity is much smaller than the velocity of light. Nevertheless, Einstein's universe is still very much determinate and objective for there exist precise mathematical rules to translate the observations of one observer to those of another, and the 'laws of nature' remain the same irrespective of the observer. The recent developments in quantum mechanics (as interpreted by Bohr, Heisenberg and others) and non-linear dynamics, however, seem to challenge the principle of determinism and the very 'objectivity' of the universe, as we shall see in the next two sections.

Implications of Quantum Theory

The simplest way to appreciate the implications of the quantum theory is perhaps through understanding of the fundamental nature of matter as revealed by quantum theory. By the beginning of twentieth century, the physicists, in their search for the fundamental building blocks of matter, had virtually reached an impasse. The process of 'breaking-up' of matter into smaller and smaller constituents ultimately led them to what are often called 'fundamental particles', like electrons, protons, neutrons, mesons etc. Naturally the very first thought was to associate these fundamental particles with something similar to classical 'particles' (let us call these as 'corpuscles', following Newton). This conceptualization was supported by the fact that these particles also have some definite rest mass and a definite charge. However, the similarity with classical 'corpuscles' ended here and it was discovered that these particles have rather strange properties. Thus, it was found that unlike classical corpuscles, where it is possible to precisely describe the state by a definite set of numbers–the coordinates and the velocity components, no precise specification of state is possible for these 'fundamental particles'[9]. Quantum theory now tells us that a fundamental particle itself cannot have simultaneously a definite coordinate and a corresponding definite momentum, the uncertainties in their magnitude being related by the famous Heisenberg's uncertainty relationship

$$\Delta p_x \, \Delta x \geq h$$

where

$\Delta x =$ the uncertainty in specification of x–coordinate of the particle

$\Delta p_x =$ the uncertainty in the specification of the x–projection of momentum of the particle

$h =$ Planck's constant $= 6.63 \times 10^{-34}$ J.s

(similar relations could also be written for the y and z coordinates).

Thus, if the microparticle is located at a certain definite point x, ($\Delta x = 0$, and therefore $\Delta p_x = \infty$), then the x–projection of its momentum must have arbitrarily large uncertainty. Similarly if its velocity is known for certain, we cannot make any statement regarding its location[10]. Clearly, for the fundamental particle the classical concept of trajectory is not applicable. From a known position of the particle at a certain time t, it is impossible to predict the value of its coordinates at the time t + dt.*

This revelation clearly cuts at the roots of classical determinism, stated succinctly in the bold assertion of Laplace quoted earlier. Laplacian determinism completely excludes the element of chance from the behaviour of an isolated object, while in quantum physics probability plays a fundamental role. In classical physics the element of chance appears only when considering aggregates of objects, for an exact description of which we would need to have much more information about the individual objects than is practically possible. Usually, we are interested only in the average behaviour of such aggregates (e.g. an aggregate consisting of the molecules of a gas) and this can be obtained by postulating suitable statistical laws without carrying out a complete solution of all the equations governing the behaviour of each individual object of the aggregate. Thus, we describe the motion of a gas by means of probability laws (the laws of statistics) but underlying them all are the exact laws of Newtonian mechanics governing the motion of each individual molecule. In quantum theory, however, we are considering the element of chance in the behaviour of a *single object*. "The elements of statistical collectives considered in quantum mechanics, are not the micro-objects themselves, but the

---

*And if we recall the facts of interconversion and spontaneous decay of fundamental particles, the dissimilarity with classical 'corpuscles' becomes even more glaring.

results of experiments with them, a definite experimental arrangement corresponding to a definite collective[11]". The probabilistic nature of phenomena at the level of fundamental particles can be understood through a simple experiment.

Let us consider electrons (typical fundamental particles) emanating from a source 1 and arriving at screen 3 after passing through a very narrow slit A in the shielding screen 2. Had the fundamental particles been like classical corpuscles, they would have all moved in a straight line till they reached the screen 3 and all of them should hit the screen at precisely the same point X in line with points 1 and A.* However, in reality it is seen that the particles arrive at the screen over a much wider area around point X, in a manner which is totally unpredictable in so far as each individual particle is concerned. However, if we allow a sufficiently large number of particles to pass through the slit, and detect the intensity of their impingement on the screen a regular distribution I (x), as shown in Fig. 1, is observed indicating that though each particle leaving A arrives at screen 3 in its 'own way', it is possible to assign a certain probability of arrival of the particle at any position x. It must be appreciated that this probabilistic description is not the result of any 'non-idealities' in the experimental set-up. We are talking of

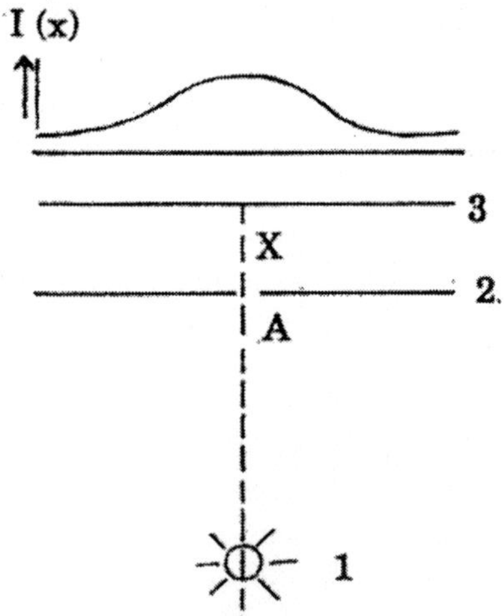

Fig. 1

* Or, if we wish to take into account the finite size of aperture A, the electrons should reproduce on the photographic plate an exact outline of the aperture. If the opening is a small hole, the photograph should reproduce a small dot and nothing more.

ideal experimental conditions – there is no wind or streams of heated air coming up from the earth that could affect the 'journey' of particles from the aperture to the screen! The probabilistic description is intrinsic to quantum mechanics. As Pauli stated in his Nobel lecture:"...the statements of quantum mechanics are dealing only with possibilities, not with actualities. They have the form, 'This is not possible', or 'Either this or that is possible', but they can never say, 'that will actually happen then and there'..."[12]

Of course, this doesn't imply that there is complete 'Indeterminacy' in quantum physics. Causality in micro-phenomena is certainly present, but it is considerably different from the classical determinism which is characteristic of the 'old physics'. In quantum mechanics, it is not the actual events, but the possibilities of their realization that are causally related[13]. Since 'possible' and 'actually realized' events are identical in classical mechanics, it is clear that upon a transition from the quantum to the classical description of the world (e.g., from micro to macro phenomena), the causal relation between the possible events must be converted into causal relation between realized events. In this sense, the quantum mechanical principle of casuality is a generalisation of the classical determinism. One is thus forced to conclude from quantum physics that the basic laws of nature are not 'deterministic' but statistical and that the probabilistic form of causality is the fundamental form while the classical determinism is just its limiting (degenerate) case!

Another very strange property of these fundamental particles is encountered when we modify the experimental set-up of Fig. 1 by making one more aperture B in the shielding screen 2, as shown in Fig. 2. When only one of the slits (either A or B) is open, the particles arrive at the screen, as expected on the basis of our previous discussion, in a manner governed by the probabilistic distribution akin to that observed in Fig. 1. Thus, the distribution with slit A open will be $I_1(x)$ centred around a point on the screen 3 in line with points 1 and A; and that with slit B open would be $I_2(x)$ centred around a point on the screen in line with points 1 and

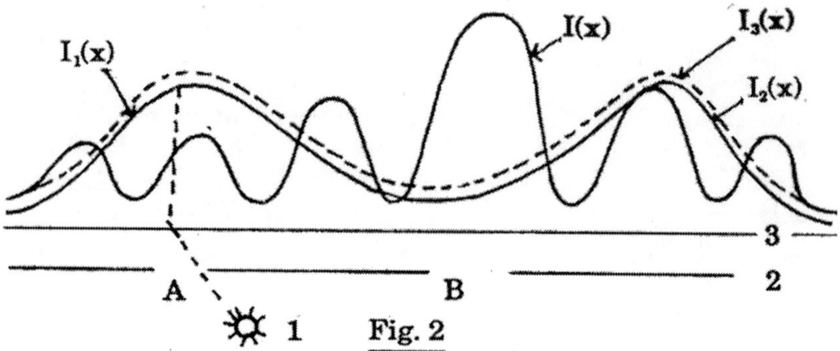

Fig. 2

B (Fig. 2). But if we open both the slits A and B, what is most amazing is that we do not get the distribution $I_1(x) + I_2(x)$, described by curve $I_3(x)$ in the diagram, but a distribution I(x) which resembles the interference pattern obtained with light or sound waves.

Two 'explanations' of this remarkable observation have been attempted by physicists, neither of which makes any classical sense(14). In the first interpretation it is said that each indivisible particle somehow manages to go through both slits at the same time and interfere with 'itself', contributing to the wave pattern on the screen, yet somehow registering as a single click. The other suggested 'explanation' is even more crazy. It is presumed that though each electron passes through only one of the slits, somehow each particle 'knows' where the particles preceding it have gone and where the ones following it will go so that at the end of the experiment they all together have piled up in a nice wave pattern for the experimenter to puzzle over; for had this not been the case, it should not have mattered for an electron passing through one slit whether the neighbouring slit is open or closed and therefore the distribution of impingement with both slits open should have followed the addition curve $I_3(x) = I_1(x) + I_2(x)$, with the particles passing through slit A contributing the portion $I_1(x)$ and those passing through slit B contributing the portion $I_2(x)$!

Clearly, both these 'explanations' are only wild interpretations, neither one actually telling anything about what this entity, that the scientists are working with, really is. In fact, the only logical conclusion arising from the existence of 'interference' is that the fundamental particles in motion also exhibit 'wave' properties. The fundamental particles are thus not 'purely' (in the classical sense) corpuscular; and at the same time they are not purely wave-like; they are something qualitatively different. A physical intuitive model of fundamental particles is, in fact, not possible, since our senses can only detect either corpuscular motion characterized by a localization of the object moving in a definite trajectory in space or wave motion characterised by the motion of the medium. It may be said that fundamental particles are to some extent akin to corpuscles and in some respects these are like waves, but unfortunately for the classical 'objectivists', even this depends not on the particles themselves but on the 'observer', specifically on the manner in which the 'observer' has arranged the apparatus of observation. Thus, recalling our earlier discussion, if a beam of electrons is made to pass through a slit in a screen, it exhibits clear 'corpuscular' properties and each electron can be actually 'observed' to hit the detector screen very much like bullets hitting the target. On the other hand, if the experimenter makes the same beam pass through two slits, an interference pattern characterising 'wave like' nature of electrons during their passage through the slits emerges. Even in this case, when impinging on the detector screen, the electrons exhibit corpuscular properties – each of them is distinctly registered at a certain point on the screen.

The fundamental particles thus don't seem to possess any 'intrinsic' nature (even a rather 'temperamental' nature) waiting to be revealed to an inquisitive observer. As summed up by Capra[15]: "My conscious decision about how to observe, say, an electron will determine the electron's properties to some extent. If I ask it a particle question, it will give me a particle answer, if I ask it a wave question, it will give me a wave answer. The electron does not have objective properties independent of my mind". The classical notion of 'objectivity' of all phenomena and the sharp Cartesian-partition between mind and matter could not ask for a subtler battering!

This realisation in fact forms the basis of one of the very important principles of quantum physics, viz., the principle of complementarity put forth by Niels Bohr. The essence of this principle lies in the following: In any experiment with microparticles the observer gets information not about the 'properties of the particles themselves' but about the properties of the particles associated with some particular situation including, among other things, the measuring instruments. The information about the objects obtained under some definite conditions should be considered as complementary to the information obtained under different conditions. Evidence obtained under different experimental conditions cannot be comprehended within a single picture, but must be regarded as various sides (complementing one another) of a single reality, to wit the object under investigation[16]. This seems to echo Kant's pronouncement that the thing in itself (*Ding an sich*) is beyond man's ken. Quantum mechanics thus reveals an intimate connection between the 'object' and the 'observer', and the absurdity of talking about objects as being 'isolated'. As Niels Bohr wrote[17], "Isolated material particles are abstractions, their properties being definable and observable only through their interaction with other systems"

Quantum physics thus cuts at the roots of the classical doctrine of reductionism. It shows that we cannot decompose the world into independently existing smallest units[18]. As we penetrate into matter, nature does not show us any isolated basic building blocks but rather appears as a complicated web of relations between the various parts of a unified whole. The subatomic particles – and therefore, ultimately, all parts of the Universe – cannot be understood as isolated entities but must be defined through their inter-relations. To quote Bohm[19], "It seems necessary to give up the idea that the world can correctly be analyzed into distinct parts, and to replace it with the assumption that the entire Universe is basically a single indivisible unit. Only in the classical limit, can the description in terms of component parts be correctly applied without reservations. Wherever quantum phenomena play a significant role, we shall find that the apparent parts can change in a fundamental way with the passage of time, because of the underlying indivisible connections between them. Thus, we are led to picture the world as an indivisible, but flexible and everchanging unit...."

Chaotic Behaviour in Newtonian Dynamics

While quantum theory points to the breakdown of classical determinism in the world of ultra-small fundamental particles, the very recent discovery of chaotic behaviour in simple dynamical systems shatters the age-old belief in the complete 'predictability' of macroscopic systems. Probably the most striking example of such 'limits to predictability' is provided by studies of John Miles[(20)] on the spherical pendulum, the moving element of a traditional wall clock. It has been shown (both experimentally and by theoretical calculations) that this pendulum system, normally thought of as an epitome of regularity, becomes chaotic if the top end, instead of being kept fixed, is forced to oscillate with a frequency slightly lower than the natural frequency of oscillation of the pendulum 'fixed' at the top. As pointed out by Lighthill[(21)], this sensational discovery shows that... 'a fundamental uncertainty about the future is there, indeed, even on the supposedly solid basis of the good old laws of motion of Newton, which effectively are the laws of motion satisfied by all macroscopic systems'[(21)]. As stressed by Lighthill, it must be appreciated that this failure of prediction is not due to...'not having formulated the right differential equations or...not employing a big enough computer to solve them precisely or...not using accurate initial conditions,'[(21)]... but due to the intrinsic nature of the laws of Newtonian dynamics. It is a 'mathematical' result based upon rigorous 'proof' in the mathematical sense. Though the equations governing the system are known exactly and are solved precisely, yet, however accurately the initial conditions may be observed prediction is still impossible beyond a certain predictability horizon.

These discoveries, which are in a sense as profound as the Heisenberg's Uncertainty Principle completely shatter the Laplacian belief in the determinism of the mechanical Universe and have led to one of the most moving statements by the doyen of practitioners of mechanics, Sir James Lighthill:" Here I...speak once again on behalf of the broad global fraternity of practioners of mechanics. We are all deeply conscious today that the enthusiasm of our forebearers for the marvellous achievements of Newtonian mechanics led them to make generalizations in this area of predictability which, indeed, we may have generally tended to believe before 1960, but which we now recognize were false. We collectively wish to apologize for having misled the general educated public by spreading ideas about the determinism of systems satisfying Newton's laws of motion, that after 1960, were to be proved incorrect."(21)

The Paradigm of 'New Physics'

Summing up our discussion of the implications of 'New Physics' we can say that the recent discoveries highlighted above are slowly bringing about a profound change in the perception of the scientists. The breakdown of classical notion of determinism has supplanted the audacious 'know-all attitude' by a more humble and reverent behaviour towards the mysterious Universe. The scientific community, by and large, now realises that the physical sciences cannot reveal the ultimate truth since these deal only with appearances and not with the reality behind these appearances. From quantum and relativity theories emerges a holistic vision of Universe as an interconnected web of dynamic relations wherein the human observer and his consciousness play a key role. Consequently, it seems impossible to get at the 'ultimate truth' of the 'observed' physical world without inquiring into the human 'observer' himself. This is in stark contrast to the mechanical philosophy of nineteenth and early twentieth century wherein reductionism (analysis by breaking into parts) and Cartesian partition (mind/matter division) occupied a pre-eminent position, and in rather surprising agreement with the intuitive vision of the sages of the east who proclaimed millennia ago about the unity of whole cosmos and the need for investigation into the 'inner reality' in order to arrive at the ultimate truth. (c.f. Chapter 6).

Recent Developments in Other Sciences

Just as the development of Newtonian mechanics resulted in an orientation of other sciences in tune with the mechanical view of the universe projected by it, the holistic vision of new physics also seems to have compelled other sciences to do a rethinking. A number of interesting books[17,23] analyzing these recent developments in various specialised sciences like biology, neurosciences, psychology etc. have been written in last few years and we shall here present, in brief, a few of these developments.

Biological Sciences

As discussed earlier in Chapter 3, the modelling of biology after the mechanical philosophy of Descartes resulted in a belief that some day it should be possible to explain all the activities of living organisms – physical, biological and even psychological – in terms of the properties of the constituent molecules. The whole science of molecular biology rests upon this basic tenet, and it has many spectacular successes to its credit. Nevertheless, during the last few decades, a number of phenomena have also come to light which are slowly forcing the biologists to doubt the validity of this claim and even biological sciences seem to suggest a paradigm shift.

Thus, it is now almost universally agreed that the mechanical conception of living organisms as individual entities localised in space and time is in error. There is a continual interaction not only between the organisms and their environments but also between organisms that are radically different. In fact, the whole science of ecology has emerged on the basis of this realisation. 'No man is an island' now appears to be a scientific fact rather than a poet's vision. It is, for example, well established that 98 per cent of the 10^{28} atoms of a typical human body are replaced annually. The carbon atoms in our body were once the part of the earth and shall be so again in future[23]. This constant interaction between living organisms has been brought out rather dramatically by Murchie[24] through an analysis of the fact that all breathing creatures share the same oxygen molecules. Simple calculations reveal that "...each breath you breathe must contain a quadrillion (10^{15}) atoms* breathed by the rest of the mankind within the past few weeks and more than a million atoms breathed personally sometime by each and any person on earth"[(24)].... This clearly creates a low frequency chain of chemical contact between all living humans and with all humans (and even other breathing creatures) of past and present. In fact, in the light of our 'new' understanding of the atomic behaviour, it would be virtually impossible to demarcate the domains of carbon atoms in the human body and those in the surrounding environment.

Concomitant with this scientific fact of continual change in our bodies is the experiential fact of 'persistence' and 'continuity' of our individuality. Molecular biologists believe that the genes are a kind of biological guarantee of our individuality. But again, it is now well established that what remains the same is not the 'stuff' of the gene – the thousands of individual carbon, Hydrogen, Oxygen and other atoms that comprise it (since these are in constant exchange with the world outside), but the pattern of the gene. Our individuality, even in the view of a hardcore molecular biologist is thus a non-material entity, an abstract pattern of arrangement of various molecules. A straight–forward generalisation of this view would be that all these 'individual patterns' are essentially parts of a 'global pattern' called the Universal Being by mystics.

A holistic world view is also emerging from the understanding of symbiotic relationships in living organisms. As pointed out by Chopra, "All living organisms display behaviour patterns that favour the whole over the interests of the individual part. Cells work not for themselves, but for the integrity of the tissue of which they are a part. Tissues likewise work in concert to maintain the integrity of organs

---

*on an average, a breath contains about 10^{22} atoms.

and organs in turn maintain the integrity of the whole organism.... Any part of a living organism is willing to die in order to protect the genetic wholeness of the larger entity."[35]

Then, there remains the enigma of so-called 'Unsolved problems of biology', viz., various well established biological phenomena like morphogenesis (i.e., coming into being of characteristic and specific form and internal structure in living organisms),* regulation (i.e. the capability to retain the overall Pattern of the organism in spite of severe interference),** and regeneration*** (whereby organisms are able to repair their damaged structure), etc...., which defy convincing explanation in terms of conventional molecular biology. Taking a cue from the fact that when physicists were not able to offer explanation for some well known phenomena (mentioned earlier in this chapter), a paradigm shift was called for, a young biologist Rupert Sheldrake has proposed a revolutionary explanation on the basis of existence of hidden morphogenetic fields which are'... analogous to the known fields of physics in that they are capable of ordering physical changes, even though they themselves cannot be observed directly,'[25] but differ radically from them in that latter depend on the actual state of the system (e.g. electromagnetic field depends on the distribution and movement of charged particles), whereas morphogenetic fields correspond to the potential state of a developing system and are already present before it takes up its final form.****

---

*e.g. coming into form of a tree out of its seed.

**e.g. if a part of an embryo is removed or a part is added, the organism continues to develop more or less normal structure. When one of the cells of a young embryo at the two celled stage is killed, the remaining cell gives rise not to half organism but to a small but whole organism (e.g. sea urchin). Conversely, the fusion of two young sea urchin embroyos result in the development of one great sea urchin.

***e.g. on slicing a flat worm, each of the pieces regenerates into the whole worm.

****The similarity of this description with the probabilistic vision of quantum mechanics is quite obvious.

According to Sheldrake[25], these morphogenetic fields are the 'blue prints' that play crucial role in the development and maintenance of the forms (and even movement and behaviour) in the Universe, quite akin to the role of the 'plan' of a house which could in a sense be regarded as a cause of the specific form of the house. Since each kind of system has its own characteristic form, each must have a specific kind of morphogenetic field. Thus the formation of an atom from its constituents (i.e. nucleus and electrons) is guided by one field, the shape of a molecule by another, and that of a cell by another. Like the systems they influence, morphogenetic fields are essentially hierarchical in their organisation, each field interlocking with others, and the field of a larger form orchestrates those of the smaller forms within it[25]. An individual human being – atoms, molecules, tissues, organs, systems – is thus composed of literally billions of fields all directed in an ascending interlocking order up to the general field that is the person[26].

These morphogenetic fields are not like abstract 'templates' stamping their eternal shape into matter, but these are continually and subtly modified by the very things they are forming through direct connection across space and time. Sheldrake calls this process by which the forms of previous systems influence the morphogenesis of subsequent similar systems as 'morphic resonance' – a phenomenon analogous to energetic resonance[27] in sound waves, electromagnetic fields etc., but differing from these in that it does not involve any energy transfer since morphogenetic fields are non-physical fields.

This theory of morphogenetic fields is able to provide successful explanation to all the 'Unsolved riddles' of biology mentioned earlier – thus morphic field helps replacement of damaged parts (regeneration), directs a whole organism to develop even from a part of embryo (regulation) and of course is responsible for directing the growth of a seed into the tree.

Sheldrake argues that morphogenetic fields are also associated with various activities of living organisms. Thus there are fields associated with cooking, farming, horse-riding, flying a jet, running the four-minute mile, bypass surgery etc. If this hypothesis is true, clearly the performance of these activities should become easier and easier as the time goes on due to strengthening of the morphogenetic field through 'morphic resonance'. For activities like cooking, farming etc. which have been performed for thousands of years the morphogenetic fields are already well established and the modifications due to 'morphic resonance' are not significant, but for comparatively newer activities like flying a jet, running the four-minute mile, climbing the Mount Everest, bypass surgery, or even learning 'new maths', the effect of past successes on future outcomes, as predicted by the theory is clearly discernible. This also explains more logically why once the first crystallization has been achieved of a new substance, it becomes much easier to repeat the experiment later on, and it continues to get easier, even though first crystallization has been done at considerable distance from the second.

Though it would be presumptuous to say that the morphogenetic field theory has been accepted by the scientific community yet, it has to be conceded that evidence in its favour is mounting. Many tests have been suggested to establish its validity through carefully controlled experiments and it remains to be seen how long it would take before we can draw definite conclusions from these tests. Nevertheless, the very fact that such a revolutionary non-mechanistic theory is a subject of serious discussion among the scientists indicates a shift in thinking towards a holistic vision of the Universe where the same morphogenetic field could be envisaged to direct not only the atoms and molecules in stones and planets but also those in plants, animals and human beings. It we agree to the morphogenetic field theory, the unity of human consciousness follows directly for "consciousness as a whole is a morphogenetic field giving a general shape to each individual's consciousness. Each individual consciousness also forms its own field, including its experiences and memories. This individual field resonates and modifies the field of human consciousness as a whole, affecting the future."[28] In a sense, each individual is thus responsible for the whole humanity, as the sages of yore have always stressed.

Neurosciences

There has always been something mysterious and awe-inspiring about the 'brain'–especially the complex human brain; and therefore, when it was discovered by neuroscientists in early decades of this century that there exist specific centres in the brain for practically every human function such as speech, vision, appetite, sleep and even memory, it was hailed as an epoch-making triumph of mechanical philosophy, for it conjured up the picture of brain as a factory with each machine or process housed in a given location. The recent discoveries are however throwing a serious challenge to this vision and neuroscience today seems to be undergoing the 'birth pangs' associated with the emergence of a new paradigm.

The most serious threat to the mechanical model of brain functions arises from numerous cases reported by neurosurgeons where even after removing a portion of the brain, the patient did not completely lose the capability usually ascribed to that part. Thus, Lashley[29] discovered that with 80 per cent of its visual cortex removed a rat could still respond to visual clues, and cats retained vision even after 98 per cent of their optic nerve was severed. In fact, there have been reported cases where the entire left half of a human brain (which is supposed to control the right half of the body) was removed surgically after an accident and yet patients were able to regain (after some time) control of the right half of the body. Most interestingly, even after removal of area of the brain traditionally held to be the 'seat' of memory, Lashley discovered that the patients were not left with any gap or 'hole' in the memory. The dexterity of the performance was often impaired but the knowledge was retained[29]. Again, as pointed out by Briggs and Peat[29], the ability to transfer learning from one limb to another also defies this mechanical view of localized brain function. A right-handed person can wrap the toes of his left foot around a crayon and write, albeit with some difficulty. If a group of cells in the left hemisphere of the brain are responsible for the art of writing, how could this ability be passed to cells in the opposite hemisphere?

All these well established observations are forcing the neuroscientists to rethink about the validity of the mechanical model of brain, and many new alternative models have been suggested. One such model, which demands a paradigm shift has been proposed by Karl Pribram using the analogy of a hologram. To appreciate this model let us first understand what a hologram is.

Hologram is a record of the interference fringes produced by an object. Figure 3 depicts a simple scheme to obtain it. A laser beam is split into two parts with the help of a half silvered glass plate A. One of these beams is incident on the object and the other acts as the reference beam. The beam scattered from the object when allowed to mix with the reference beam produces an interference pattern (hologram) which can be recorded on photographic plate. Using this hologram it is possible to reproduce a three-dimensional image of the object by shining the reference beam on to the plate and viewing it from the other side. The most amazing property of this hologram, however, is that even if we irradiate only a small part of it with the same reference beam we get an image, not of a part of the original object, but of the whole object itself (of course the image is not as sharp as with the complete hologram).

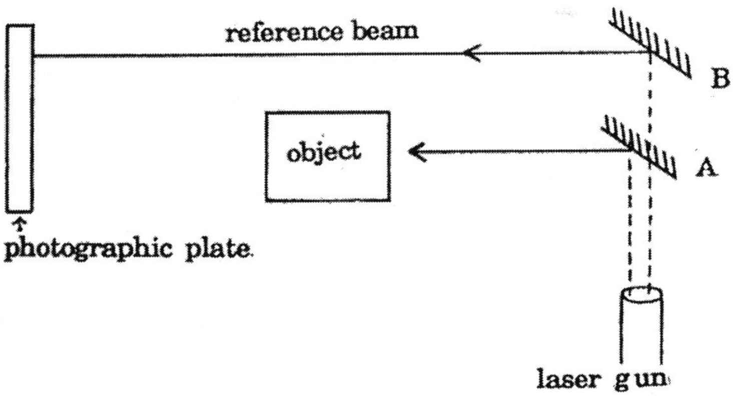

Fig. 3

It is this well known property of the hologram which suggested to Pribram the holographic model of brain function,* for if brain was a hologram every part of it would encode the same information (though with lesser clarity) as the whole. Consequently, as long as even a small part of it was intact it should be theoretically possible to retain all the functions of the brain, albeit with reduced efficiency. Pribram has not remained content with the obvious appeal of this model, and detailed mechanism of how brain could encode information (using the electrochemical activity at the junction between neurons) holographically has also been suggested[30].

The implications of this holographic model are quite profound. Not only does it negate the traditional reductionistic model, but it even goes beyond the system's view and suggests that holonomy – the whole being somehow contained in each of its parts – may be a property of the nature. As mentioned in Chapter 6, such an idea plays an important role in many mystical visions of reality.

Medicine and Health Care

The medical practitioners too are now slowly beginning to realise (albeit because of increasing incidences of 'iatrogenic'** diseases) that the traditional mechanistic model of disease as a malfunctioning of a specific human organ (like liver, kidney, spleen, stomach, lungs etc.) is inadequate. Consequently more attention is now being paid to so-called 'holistic' approaches to health care like Ayurveda, Naturopathy, Chinese medicine, Homeopathy etc., which recognise the human organism as an integrated whole and disease as an 'imbalance' in this 'whole' with respect to the nature of which it is a part. Even within conventional allopathic practice, techniques like stress relaxation, Yoga, bio-feedback have been incorporated in response to incontrovertible evidence that emotional and psychological factors or psychophysiolog-

---

* specially for visual perception

** iatrogenic diseases : diseases caused by physicians, e.g. those due to 'side–effects' associated with medicines administered to cure a specific ailment

ical connection, as Chopra [35] puts it, play a great role in the incidence of diseases like hypertension, heart attack, obesity, gastro-intestinal disorders, sexual inadequacy, insomnia, depression and even cancer. The Simontonian[31] approach to management of cancer is probably the best example of this trend.

Numerous investigations by Carl Simonton and others have established that prolonged stress is a key factor responsible for cancer growth through hormonal imbalance and suppression of person's immune system. While the former causes an increased production of abnormal cells, the latter results in failure to recognise and destroy these abnormal cells. Consequently the growth of these abnormal cells continues unabated and they soon develop into a malignant tumour – the Cancer. Simonton recognised this fact that cancer is not just a physical problem but a problem of the 'whole' person, and evolved a holistic therapy which does not focus on the disease alone but deals with the total human being. Capra[32] gives the details of their approach in a perspicuous manner. Briefly put, it involves, besides physical therapy to destroy cancer cells, strengthening the immune system through relaxation and biofeedback, psychological counselling and psychotherapy to help remove the roots of stress and even confronting the patient with the fundamental existential problems of goals in life, reasons for living, relation to the cosmos as a whole, and dealing with death – a truly holistic approach!

Psychology

As we saw in Chapter 3, the emergence of mechanistic psychology modelled after Newtonian picture of Universe as a giant machine, was a prime factor responsible for instilling faith in the materialistic worldview. It therefore seems natural that the revolutionary changes in Physics should provoke psychologists to have a relook at their studies of human behaviour. Consequently, last two decades have witnessed the emergence of a new school of psychology, termed humanistic psychology[33,34], which could usher a new worldview to replace the materialistic world view currently entrenched in our society. It recognises the utility of behaviouristic approach in understanding the traits we share with animals, but points out that there also exist other characteristics like compassion, self esteem, creativity, humour etc. which are the exclusive privileges of human beings. It looks upon man as not just a clothed tailless animal but a purposive and creative individual continuously engaged in meaningful activities of choosing, judging and organising. Thus, besides the basic material needs (like food, clothing, shelter, security, and safety) there exist a whole spectrum of the so-called 'higher' needs which manifest sequentially after the lower needs are relatively satisfied. Maslow[34] categorises these as the social needs (like belongingness, affection, acceptance, self-esteem, esteem by others), followed by moral or self–actualisation needs (like love, truth, service, justice, perfection, aesthetics, meaningfulness etc.) which result in manifestation of our inner potential. The psychological development of human beings in this model has a dynamic perspective demanding a continual shift of needs from the material ones to the higher needs of self-actualization. Any obstruction to this 'natural' emergence of higher needs causes blockage of growth and manifests as materialism, viz., excessive preoccupation with objects or egotism (self-aggrandisement and insatiable hunger for power and status). The humanistic psychology thus restores the importance due to the inner life of man and recognises that true development (and happiness) does not end with satisfaction of material needs – as the materialistic worldview proclaims, but begins there as higher needs emerge sequentially thereafter, culminating in the needs for self-actualization.

An immediate consequence of humanistic psychology is the recognition of inter-relatedness of an individual with the social and cultural environment, and this has even taken a practical shape. Psychotherapists now prefer 'group' and 'family' therapies to 'individual' therapies. Thus modern psychology further reinforces the vision that Universe is an indivisible whole, not only at the material level (through interaction of atoms and molecules) but also at the psychic level through social and cultural interaction.

Further, just as mechanistic psychology strengthened the materialistic world-view, humanistic psychology suggests that true human happiness lies in holistic development embracing all the dimensions of human personality – physical, emotional, intellectual and spiritual (the culmination of self-actualization).

NOTES

1. de Laplace, P.S., *A Philosophical Essay on Probabilities*, Dover, NY, 1952.
2. Rydnik, V., *ABC of Quantum Mechanics*, Mir Publisher Moscow, 1965, p. 18....

   A fascinating little book which presents the essential features of quantum mechanics in a simple language.
3. Kuhn, Thomas, *The Structure of Scientific Revolutions*, Chicago : Univ. of Chicago Press, 1976.
4. Minkowski, H : quoted in (2), p. 175.
5. Capra, F. *The Tao of Physics*, Fontana Collins, 1976, p. 177.

   Capra's celebrated book was the very first to bring out the philosophic import of various recent developments in the field of science and demonstrate their striking resemblance with Eastern mystical thought.
6. Good, R.H., *Basic Concepts of Relativity*, Affiliated East-West Press, New Delhi, 1974.

   This book contains a simple exposition of some of the intricate concepts of relativity through a number of well thought-out examples. The following numerical example taken from this book, serves to illustrate some of the very basic conclusions emerging from the relativity theory :

   Suppose an astronaut blasts off in the year 2000 and achieves a velocity of 2.6×10^8 m/s. Before the blastoff he was 2m tall, 0.3 m in dia, 100 kg in mass and his watch kept correct time. What are the corresponding characteristics when he is in rapid motion?

   According to the theory of relativity the contraction in the length of an object, the dialation of its time, as well as the increase in the mass of the object is by a factor γ which is related to v, the velocity of the object as measured by the observer through the expression

   $$\gamma = \frac{1}{\sqrt{1-\beta^2}}, \beta = \frac{v}{c}$$

   where c is the speed of light and equals 3×10^8 m/sec.

   In this particular example $v = 2.6 \times 10^8$ m/sec, and

   hence $\beta = \frac{v}{c} = \frac{2.6}{3} = .87$

and $\gamma = \frac{1}{\sqrt{1-\beta^2}} = \frac{1}{\sqrt{1-.75}} = 2.0$

Thus if the astronaut is standing in the direction of motion, he is now only 1m tall instead of 2m (since $\gamma = 2$), but his diameter remains 0.3m since it is transverse to his velocity. If, on the other hand, he is lying down, then his height is still 2m but his thickness is only .15m in the direction of motion. In either case, his mass is now 200 kg instead of 100 kg at earth, and his watch also runs slow by a factor of 2. If, for example, he returns in 40 years, i.e. in 2040 A.D, he will only be 20 years older, rather than 40 years, in terms of his own bodily functions, because every function must slow down in the same proportion. His heartbeat, for example, is like the ticking of a clock and like any other clock, it must run slow when moving rapidly with respect to observers back on the earth.

One may be tempted to ask the question, "After all, if the astronaut has travelled with respect to the earth, the earth too has travelled with respect to the astronaut. Shouldn't the clocks on earth too slow down as seen by the astronaut?"

The answer is that astronaut's frame of reference is not an inertial one (ie., it is not in which Newton's first law of motion holds) since he has to undergo an acceleration to get back to the earth. Special Theory of relativity is applicable only to inertial reference frames and the calculations for non-inertial frame involve general relativity theory. And it turns out that the acceleration affects the astronaut's observations in such a manner that at the end of the voyage he agrees that the earth has aged more than he has!

7. Good, R.H., ibid., p. 12

The following example brings out this point clearly. As shown in the figure, two trains of equal length are passing each other going in opposite directions with equal speeds. An observer, who is stationary with respect to earth finds that the trains are equally shrunk (by factor of mentioned above), so he observes (after correction for the finite speed of light) that end A passes end A′ at the same time that B passes B′. On the other hand, an

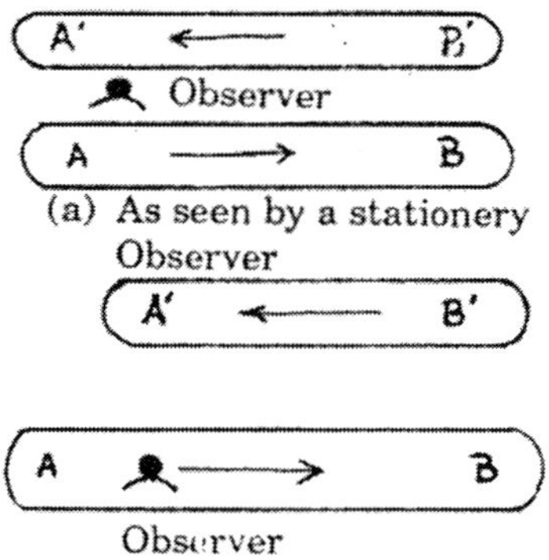

(a) As seen by a stationery Observer

(b) As seen by an Observer on a Train

Fig. Trains of Equal Length Passing Fig. 4

observer in the rightward moving train finds that the other train is shorter (because γ factor applies to the other train and not to his); and so he observes that ends B's pass each other before A's do. Thus events that are simultaneous in one frame of reference are not necessarily simultaneous in another.

In high energy physics involving interactions between particles moving close to the speed of light, this relativity of time has been verified by numerous experiments.

8. Capra, Fritzof : op.cit., p. 81

9. Tarasov, L.V., *Basic Concepts of Quantum Mechanics*, Mir Publishers, Moscow, 1980.

   This book gives a detailed and systematic exposition of the fundamentals of basic quantum physics. The discussion of wave-particle duality and some of the basic experiments with 'fundamental particles' are especially revealing.

10. Tarasov, L.V., ibid, p. 35.

11. Fock, V.A., quoted in Tarasov, L.V., ibid., p. 120.

12. Pauli, W., quoted in Tarasov, L.V., ibid., p. 118.

13. Since in any practical situation we only deal with events that have been realized, a question may naturally arise regarding the utility of such a causality which only relates the possibilities of realization of events rather than the events themselves. The answer to this question is as follows :

    The observer must repeat a set of similar acts of measurements (for this he must have a sufficiently large number of similar microparticles, ensuring each time the same external conditions for each of them). In each act of measurement a random value of the quantity being measured will be realized. However, a set of these random values will allow us to find the law of distribution and the mean value of the quantity which can be predicted *a priori*. The existence of a causal relationship between possible events is expressed through the possibility of such predictions.

    ...(from Tarasov, L.V. ibid, p. 118,)

14. Briggs, J.P. and F. David Peat, *Looking Glass Universe–The Emerging Science of Wholeness*, Fontana Paperbacks, 1985, p. 53.

15. Capra, Fritjof : op.cit., p. 77.

16. Tarasov, L.V., op cit, p. 152.

17. Quotation of Niels Bohr in Capra, Fritjof : *The Turning Point – Science society and the rising culture*, Flamingo, Fontana paperback, 1983, p. 69

... A sequel to the earlier book *The Tao of Physics* by Capra gives a detailed discussion of the new paradigm emerging from recent developments in physics, biology, health care, psychology etc.

18. The rejection of classical individualization of an object is quite fundamental in quantum physics, being also a direct outcome of the Uncertainty Principle. In classical mechanics, objects are known to have individuality since it is always possible in principle to enumerate them and observe precisely the behaviour of any one of them. In this case, however alike two classical objects may be, they are never identical and can always be distinguished—a privilege denied to fundamental particles, for which, as discussed earlier, there is no trajectory so that even if we were to isolate and 'label' an electron at the instant t = 0, it does not have the individuality which would allow it to be identified in the assembly of electrons after a certain time t. Consequently two microparticles of the same type should be treated as absolutely identical. Thus, all electrons are identical and so are all unexcited hydrogen atoms, helium nuclei etc.

    The indistinguishability of fundamental particles is responsible for basic difference between usual statistical laws (valid for distinguishable alternatives) and the quantum statistics. This has been used to explain the 'anamolous' behaviour of particles in the experimental set up of Fig. 2 (Tarasov, L.V. op.cit., pp. 79-114).

19. Bohm. D. quoted in Tarasov, L.V. op.cit., p. 62.

20. Miles, John., Physica D11, 1984, p. 309.

21. Lighthill, J. : *The recently recognized failure of predictability in Newtonian Dynamics*, Proc. Royal Society, London, vol. 407, A, pp. 35-50 (1986).

22. Briggs, J.P. and F.D. Peat : *Looking Glass Universe–The Emerging Science of Wholeness*, Fontana paperback, Glasgow, 1985.

    As suggested by the subtitle, this interesting book presents a detailed analysis of quantum and relativity theories, Bohm's theory of implicate order, Prigogine's theory of emergence of order out of chaos, Jantsch's theory of self-organising systems, Sheldrake's morphogenetic field theory and Pribram's holographic model of brain, all of which point to a holistic vision of the world.

23. Dossey, Larry : *Space, Time and Medicine*, Shambhala, London, 1982.,p. 74.

    An interesting book which talks about developments in medicine in the light of new understanding of space-time relationship emerging from new physics.

24. Murchie, quoted in Dossey, Larry, op. cit., p. 76.

25. Sheldrake, Rupert : *A New Science of Life : The hypothesis of formative causation*Collins, London, 1988.

26. Briggs, J.P. and F.D. Peat : *Looking Glass Universe*...op.cit., p. 237.

27. Resonance: is the phenomenon of intensification of amplitudes of vibrations when the natural frequency of the vibrating system coincides with the excitation frequency.

    Thus, when an army of marching soldiers is crossing a suspension bridge, if the natural frequency of oscillation at bridge coincides with the frequency at their steps, the bridge will undergo dangerously large oscillations.

28. Briggs. J.P. and F.D. Peat, op.cit., p. 250.

29. ibid pp. 262-264.

30. ibid pp. 277-285.

31. Simonton, O.C., et al. : *Getting Well Again, Los Angles,* Tarcher, 1978.

    ...Gives a detail description of Simonton's holistic approach to Cancer Management.

32. Capra, Fritjof, *The Turning Point*, op.cit., pp. 390-391.

33. Maslow, Abraham : *Towards a Psychology of Being*, Princeton : Van Nostrand Reinhold, 1962.

34. Maslow, Abraham : *Motivation and Personality*, New York, Harper & Row, 1970.

35. Chopra, Deepak: *Creating Health: Beyond Prevention, Towards Perfection*, Grafton Books, Collins, 1989, p 159.

6 RE-EMERGENCE OF THE ESSENCE OF HUMANISM

The eschewing of all evil, the perfecting of noble deeds, the purifying of one's mind, this is the teaching of the enlightened ones.

Buddha
(Dhammapada, Verse 183)

As discussed at length in Chapter 3, the rise of the materialistic paradigm was preceded by general decadence of religion which became more and more dogmatic and full of rituals and superstitions. With progressive entrenchment of materialistic philosophies, the essence of religion got completely eclipsed. In such an environment of stark materialism, even the humanistic impulses that emerged (e.g. Marxism) confined themselves to materialistic welfare of people.

While more or less the whole world had come in the grip of Western materialistic domination and materialism had became the cult of humanity, there appeared signs of a rediscovery of the true basis of humanism in India. Pitched against the most dominant political power of the British Imperialism, India, during her freedom struggle was forced to dig deep to tap strength from it's long neglected storehouse of ancient wisdom. Thus, a sort of spiritual renaissance sprouted in India and spread to the West. It became conspicuous towards the end of 19th century. A number of spiritual giants such as Swami Vivekananda, Swami Ram Tirth, Sri Aurobindo and others appeared to broadcast once again the essence of religion in its pristine form. Also, Mahatama Gandhi demonstrated the miracle of non-materialistic paradigm by using Ahimsa as a successful weapon in the freedom struggle. More recently, a number of spiritual movements have emerged from India and have become popular in the Western world as well. This renaissance of ancient wisdom has been a potent factor contributing towards the emergence of the new world view. In this chapter, we shall attempt to understand what this ancient wisdom is and how it forms the bedrock of humanism. However, to prepare ground for this understanding, we briefly recall the basic fallacy of the materialistic paradigm.

Basic Flaw of the Materialistic Paradigm

The fundamental tenet of the materialistic paradigm is the belief that material interaction is the prime source of human happiness. In consonance with this belief, maximization of material prosperity and material comforts becomes the most cherished objective and the indicators of progress are decided accordingly. Human happiness becomes synonymous with material welfare. An immediate corollary to this definition of happiness is that if we can establish a foolproof system to promote material prosperity and to safeguard it adequately, peace and happiness will be ensured. To understand the fallacy of this premise, let us go deeper into the mechanism of happiness resulting from material interactions.

(a) If happiness is an objective outcome of material interactions, it logically follows that any given interaction should produce the same amount of happiness irrespective of any other condition.

We all know this to be incorrect, from our own personal experiences, for the intensity of enjoyment reduces with successive interactions. In fact, depending upon the state of mind even the most enjoyable interaction may become intolerable. Happiness seems to be more directly related to the state of mind, rather than to the material interactions.

(b) All material interactions, howsoever pleasant these may be, are transient, while the urge for happiness is unending. Therefore, any shortlived pleasant experience leaves a craving in the mind to perpetuate it. Thus, the more one 'enjoys' the sensory pleasures, the more one desires to do so again. Gradually, one develops an addiction and is utterly miserable when that pleasure cannot be made available. In addition, too much indulgence degenerates the senses, the very instruments of deriving material pleasure.

(c) Our instruments of material enjoyment are prone to the inevitable natural process of aging and, therefore, the capability of enjoyment is, perforce, snatched away from us with age. With senses degenerating and the addiction increasing, one becomes a helpless victim of materialism.

Thus we see that pursuit of happiness through material pleasures is a mirage which ultimately leads us to misery. It is, therefore, very important to understand what the source of real happiness is and why we fall into the trap of materialism.

In this context, men of great wisdom proclaimed that the happiness which we ascribe to material interactions is, in fact, a consequence of temporary quietening of the agitation created in our minds prior to the material interaction due to craving for that interaction. This craving is, in turn, the result of our 'instinctive' response to the sensations continually arising in our body due to interactions of various senses (including the thoughts in the mind) with the surroundings. The Buddha put it this way:

"Here one sees a visual object; it is pleasant, one is attracted, if it is unpleasant, one is repelled. Similarly with sounds, smells, tastes, bodily contacts and mental objects (i.e. thoughts, volitions, emotions, etc.): If they are pleasant, one is attracted, if they are unpleasant, one is repelled...one who lives thus swayed by likes and dislikes, whenever he experiences a sensation—pleasant, unpleasant or neutral—he reacts by welcoming and enjoying the pleasure and grows attached to it...and so the desire for enjoyment arises in him. And desire for enjoyment causes clinging[1]".

The satisfaction of a desire through appropriate material interaction makes the mind temporarily quiet and free from any desire resulting in an experience of 'joy' or happiness till another desire arises and agitates the mind. The happiness thus emerges to be a characteristic of quiet and desire-free (usually termed as pure) mind or pure consciousness—a state which is independent of material interactions. In fact, it is obvious from above discussions that maximising pleasant material interactions in an attempt to eternalise this temporary gratification is selfdefeating. The only sure way to achieve permanent happiness or bliss is—we are advised by sages of all times—to purify the mind of its multifarious desires (both the desire to avoid unpleasant interactions and the desire to maximise pleasant interactions), so that instead of reacting impulsively to various situations it always remains equanimous and thus remains in its natural state of bliss. Such a pure and equanimous mind, we are told, has also the intrinsic characteristic of Universal Love and Compassion—a disinterested love of one's fellow beings which spontaneously motivates one to seek their good and happiness without desiring anything for oneself. Humanism or concern for welfare of all human beings is thus a natural outcome of purification of mind, since a pure mind automatically experiences the fact that there is only one Reality immanent in the whole universe; as Buddha put it, "...that man there is thou".

These assertions of sages are borne out of their own experiences based on years of painstaking research and effort at purifying their minds and their lives are testimony to the correctness of their understanding of the nature of true happiness.

Yet, in modern times when materialistic worldview is reigning supreme, we find it difficult to believe that to be in bliss is the 'natural' state of human beings for we rarely find ourselves in that state. The reason for this situation is our ignorance about true nature of happiness and the nature of human reality itself which keeps on getting strengthened by our day-to-day interactions in the world. Right from the birth, the tendency of the senses being outward going, one is all the time engaged in interaction with the outside world. Even when we are thinking, it is always about our interaction with the objects. As a result of this, one is continuously exposed to the agitations of pleasant and unpleasant interactions. The usual tendency of the mind being to seek pleasure, these interactions reinforce the mental impressions *(Samskaras)* of craving and aversion, and thus continuously strengthen the trap of ignorance and misery. In such a frame of sensory perception, one's notion about oneself also gets completely distorted. Thus, one gets engrossed with the notion that the human reality comprises of the body-mind-intellect mechanism. As body is the outermost part and the most tangible one in the sensory perception, all the characteristics of body are misconceived to be the characteristics of the human reality. Thus, 'I am the body', 'I am the mind' etc. become the guiding directions in our conduct of life. Since in such a state of ignorance, the only source of happiness that we experience is through certain types of body-mind interactions, our identity with body and mind is complete and we become totally oblivious of our true nature—the nature of pure consciousness free from body-mind agitations.

In this way, every one in this world is prone to the above illusion and a victim of the misery trap woven by it. Only by a sustained effort to acquire correct intellectual understanding and subsequently by an arduous and painstaking attempt to purify the mind of all desires, one can liberate oneself from this trap and discover the secret of true happiness.

Our close identification with body-mind phenomena, it may be argued, is the sole cause of all negativities. Thus, by identification with the body, one foolishly imagines oneself to be changeful, subject to death and decay, localised and confined within the boundaries of the body. Fear, insecurity, selfishness are the direct outcomes. The colour and the stature of the body become factors to make one feel elated or depressed whereas the true characteristics of human being are those of permanent bliss. It is *sat-chit-ananda.* viz., existence-awareness-bliss absolute! And 'Thou art that', proclaim the scriptures.

One can easily visualise the enormous difference that exists between these two perceptions. It becomes obvious that to move towards the correct perception should be the sole purpose of human life. This is the only way to emancipate oneself from the ever-engulfing misery trap in which we all are caught up.

Realization of one's unity with the whole universe, as mentioned earlier, is the essence of humanism and progenitor of all human values such as honesty, compassion, love, sacrifice, non-violence etc. For, as declared majestically in Isa Upanisad, *"Yastu sarvani bhutani atmanyevanupasyati; sarvabhutesu catmanam tato na vijugupsate"* *

* यस्तु सर्वाणि भूतानि आत्मन्येवानुपश्यति।
सर्वभूतेषु चात्मानं ततो न विजुगुप्सेत।।

"The wiseman, who realises all beings as not distinct from his own self, and his own self as the self of all beings does not, by virtue of that perception, hate anyone".

"Yasmin sarvanibhutani atmaivabhut vijanatah, tatra ko mohah kah sokah ekatvam anupasyatah" **

** यस्मिन्स र्वाणि भूतानि आत्मैवाभूद्विजानतः।
तत्र को मोहः कः शोकः एकत्वं अनुपश्यतः।।

"What delusion, what sorrow can there be for that wise man who realizes the unity of all existence by perceiving all beings as his own self?"[2] Only through such an understanding can there be an end to the evergrowing strife in the human psyche which is impelled on one side by strong samskaras of ignorance accumulated through long sensory experience, and on the other, by the pangs of conscience demanding obeisance to truth.

Only a person endowed with such an understanding will be able to justify for himself the logic of self-sacrifice for the good of others and will be able to abide by the notion of universal brotherhood. In the light of such an understanding, exploitation for material accumulation, consumerism, attachment to family bonds, hankering after name and fame will all appear to be utterly futile and self-defeating.

Unless we strive for such a realization, attempts to build harmony with nature, ecological balance, peace and nonviolence will remain superficial.

This is the quintessence of ancient wisdom. How to actualize it in practice is the important question which will be discussed in the next chapter.

NOTES

1. Amadeo Sole'-Leris, "Tranquility and Insight", Shambhala Press, Boston, 1986, p. 16.

   This book contains a lucid account of the Buddhist Meditation according to the oldest tradition and as a living practice in our time.

2. Swami Ranganathananda, "The Message of the Upanisads",
   Bhartiya Vidya Bhavan, Bombay, 1987, p. 108

   This book based on the lectures delivered by Swami Ranganathananda on three Principal Upanisads viz., Isa-,Kena- and Katho-panisad is a masterly exposition of the subtle Vedanta philosophy.

7 METHODS OF INNER DEVELOPMENT

Each soul is potentially divine.

The goal is to manifest this Divinity within by controlling nature, external and internal; do this either by work, or worship, or psychic control or philosophy—by one, or more, or all of these and be free.

This is the whole of Religion. Doctrines or dogmas or rituals or books or temples or forms are but secondary details.

Swami Vivekananda

The oriental sages weren't satisfied by just pointing out the fallacy of materialistic notion of happiness. Being practical philosophers, and moved by compassion for the suffering masses, they developed practical techniques which enabled ordinary men and women to purify their minds and overcome the stubborn, but false identification with Body-Mind-Intellect (B-M-I) complex and thus experience the innate joy—the bliss which is the birthright of all human beings. The references to such techniques are found scattered in the ancient spiritual literature of India—the Upanisads, Sermons of the Buddha, Patanjali's Yoga Darshan, the Bhagwad-Gita, the Bhagwatam, the Yoga Vasistha and numerous other works.

In modern times, it was Swami Vivekananda who first presented a coherent picture of all these methods. The sages of the yore developed these techniques according to the need of the times and the temperament of people, and it is therefore not surprising that at a cursory glance these methods appear quite different, sometimes even contradictory. Vivekananda pointed out that these approaches—like different routes to reach a mountain peak—though outwardly quite different, lead to the same goal.

This process of inner (or spiritual) development has traditionally been called 'Yoga'—a Sanskrit word meaning 'to unite' or 'to merge', the implication in the present context being merger of apparent illusive 'individual self' with the real, 'Universal Self'. Vivekananda[2] categorised various techniques into four broad categories, viz.,

1. Jnana Yoga — The method of reason
2. Karma Yoga — The method of selfless activity
3. Bhakti Yoga — The method of devotion
4. Raj Yoga — The method of mind control and meditation

Jnana Yoga:

In this method one uses reason and logic to understand the true nature of reality. The chief strategy is to identify the non-self starting from the outer-most sheath of the body. As one analyses the characteristics of the body through logical arguments and examples, conviction is developed and reinforced that:

(a) body is not the real Me, it is non-self,

(b) the body is changing every moment. The appearance of form and colour and the fact that the change in body from moment to moment is almost imperceptible, is responsible for creating the illusion 'I am the body'. Accumulated over a long period, even this infinitesimal rate of change produces drastic results and the false identification of 'I' with the body becomes intellectually obvious.

In a similar manner, the nature of the mind is then analyzed. Varieties of procedures have been suggested for this purpose, but probably the most effective one (employed in modern times by Ramana Maharshi[(3)]) consists of focusing the mind on the enquiry–who am I? As soon as a thought or any other changeful, identifiable trait of mind is observed, immediately one becomes conscious—this is not me. The attempt is not to do anything but to calmly and silently observe, first the body and then the mind, and to negate the non-self as soon as it becomes the object of experience. This process continued over a long period takes one more and more within oneself. With a sharp and steady discrimination unshaken by the pleasures and pains experienced (for these too are not real) one keeps on developing one's wisdom—'Panya' as Buddha called it-to discriminate the non-self from the self which is actually the cogniser of all experiences. As more and more attention is focussed towards the self, layer after layer of impurities of the superimposition are peeled off. The mind becomes sharper and purer and the internal bliss is experienced more and more with the result that the attraction of sensory pleasures and the aversion or fear of outside pain tends to loosen its grip. The seeker then works with much more determination to shed off the illusion completely. Observing various sheaths of the mind and remaining absorbed in the process for a long time, one even loses the feeble tendency to look for 'something'. One develops the understanding that actually this very tendency to 'look for something' other than the self is responsible for the illusive perception. Therefore, finally a state is reached when the 'seer' gets merged in the self. There is no seeing now in the normal sense, i.e. in the context of subject-object duality. There is only one single, infinite, unchanging Blissful Existence which is the ultimate reality. Returning from such a state one is totally liberated from the B-M-I identification, and appearance of duality does not baffle him anymore. The seeker becomes the 'seer', for he can now continually experience the 'underlying unity' in the variegated existence. The whole Universe becomes for him, the play of Brahman—the single all pervading unity.

Karma Yoga (the path of selfless service)

This is the path of self-realization advocated in the Gita by Lord Krishna. It is particularly suited for people who believe in vigorous action and is also helpful in making our day-to-day activity a means of self-realization. It primarily emphasizes detachment from the fruit of action: "The right is to work only, but never to its fruits; let not the fruit of action be thy motive nor let thy attachment be to inaction".

The essential implications of this injunction are twofold. Firstly, it clearly follows that the actions should be inspired by noble altruistic motives, for it would be impossible to be free from anxieties and fears about the fruits of actions if these are propelled by narrow personal gains. Secondly, even such noble actions should be performed with such an inspired self- forgetfulness that no thoughts of the 'rewards of action' are entertained. The work itself becomes the reward and whatever be the 'physical' consequences of the action, the 'doer' maintains his equanimity. Now, since all actions are basically propelled by the past predispositions (samskaras or vasanas)* and will bear either pleasant or bitter fruit, maintenance of equanimity towards the results of action results in purgation of these samskaras. Giving up enjoyership of the fruits of action is a natural precursor to abdication of doership and false identification with B-M-I complex. In this manner the mind becomes purer, steadfast and slowly the addiction to outside pleasures vanishes, one automatically tends to draw in and feel the Inner Bliss. By such an attitude to work, all interactions with outside world become a help to move out of the illusion rather than becoming a means of strengthening ignorance. One is not propelled to work for the sake of pleasant results. Freedom from samskaras and not

---

* The Sanskrit word samskara refers to the impressions of our experiences on the mind. These samskaras are alive in the sense that they have in them the power to recreate the entire experience which caused them in the first instance. In fact each impression seeks a repetition of the corresponding original experience[(5)].

enjoyment becomes the motivation to work. All work in such a case becomes purifier and a source of inner development. Finally, it may be emphasized that as the notion of "doer" and 'enjoyer' becomes feeble, one percieves oneself as an inseparable part of the 'whole' Reality—thus moving towards the Truth as explained in the last section.

Bhakti Yoga (the Path of Devotion)

This path involves proper channelisation of human emotions which are usually directed unintelligently towards a limited circle of people and often blended with strong instinctive propensities, such as greed, anger, lust etc. strengthening the body-mind illusion. It also defiles the mind by creation of attraction towards some and hatred for others. But if the emotions are harnessed to move towards the real self-usually anthropomorphised into a Divine Being, Prophet or a Guru with an attitude of complete surrender and devotion, the results are just the opposite. As one starts giving more and more importance to the Divine, the importance attached to the B-M-I complex is reduced. The devotee dedicates all his life and actions to the Divine; with Him he seeks to commune in prayer, song and meditation; and Him he seeks to serve through all His creatures. The life of a devotee is thus completely suffused with love for the 'Adored One' leaving no avenue for defilement of mind due to any aversion or craving. Pure love, unlike attachment, is non-possessive and seeks nothing in return, and therefore does not give rise to craving. A true devotee looks at everyone and everything as a manifestation of the Divine and is ever eager to merge his own identity with the Divine. Thus, he constantly turns his mind away from the apparent duality. As and when any defilement arises in the mind (due to the samskaras accumulated in the past), the true devotee seeks Divine help to overcome it, and the very act of mindful surrender purges the mind of the impurity. Gradually as the mind becomes purified, the convictions about benevolence and omnipotence of the Divine are strengthened. The surrender becomes more and more 'complete' and the ego gets progressively dissolved till the devotee 'experiences' the existence of the only One.

It is pertinent to point out that the practice of idol-worship which is widely prevalent in the Indian traditions of Bhakti-Yoga is a very useful aid to reorient one's emotions in the initial stages of inner development. A human form to which the attributes of the 'Divine' are associated, serves to be a tangible, objective model for the beginner to focus his emotions. However, it is very important to use such a model intelligently and not as a superstition, so that finally the Divine is identified within one's own self.

The path of devotion or surrender is the principal methodology of spiritual development enjoined by Hinduism, Christianity and Islam (the word Islam in fact means to surrender). Indian spiritual tradition is resplendent with examples of numerous true devotees like Chaitanya, Surdas, Tulsidas, Mirabai, Ramakrishna Paramahansa etc. whose lives continue to serve as beacon lights for all spiritual aspirants.

Raja Yoga (Path of mind control and meditation)

This method addresses itself directly to the mental processes (in a manner akin to that adopted by a modern scientist in understanding the external reality) in order to prevent the formation of samskaras of craving, aversion and delusion right at the time of their origin. The emphasis is on developing awareness of the highly 'transient' nature of all samskaras. As the formation of the new samskaras is stopped, the old accumulated samskaras manifest themselves as some body-mind phenomena and if we just observe these equanimously, knowing pretty well their basic transient nature, the futility of all desires becomes clear, and the mind becomes purer. This process of direct observation of the mind, taking the bull by the horns, as it were, is obviously extremely effective but at the same time, quite demanding. Investigation into the subtler domains of mind is quite an arduous process requiring training under careful guidance.

The very first step towards these investigations is to bring the mind to a state of relative quietitude. This necessitates observance of certain basic codes of ethics and morality (Yama and Niyama, as Patanjali[6] calls them, or the

Panchsheel of the Buddha[7]) like refraining from telling a lie, stealing, indulging in sexual misconduct and using intoxicants etc. It must be appreciated that a sincere attempt at strict conformity to these codes of morality is important because wilful violation of any of these codes causes violent agitation in the mind impeding the process of quietening the mind, thus stopping further progress.

Having made a firm determination to observe these codes of morality in all sincerity, one can initiate the process of reducing the restlessness which seems to have become a 'normal' characteristic of our mind. Since the mind and the body are inextricably linked, we begin by sitting quietly in a comfortable posture—preferably crosslegged with spinal column in vertical position (since this enables us to remain mentally alert for a long time and the subtle nerve currents which are carriers of psychic energy are not obstructed). In order to reduce distractions from sensory interactions, we close our eyes, and try to choose a place for meditation which is free from noise, excessive light, heat etc.

After these preliminary steps, we can begin the actual process of quietening the mind. This can be done in a variety of ways and different meditative traditions prescribe different procedures, but almost all of them are based on the strong inter-relationship between the breathing process and the state of mind. It is one of the unique discoveries of the oriental sages that if we make the breathing process rhythmic and soft, the mind automatically becomes quieter. Since breathing can be voluntarily regulated the above discovery suggests a procedure to quieten the mind. The regulation of breath can be achieved in a variety of ways, and accordingly there exist numerous systematic procedures like Pranayama of Patanjali[6], Aana-paan (non-reactive observation of breath) of the Buddha[7], Rhythmic breathing along with recitation of a word (Mantra) etc. Each of these approaches has its special characteristics and the reader is advised to refer to the literature[6-7] dealing with these techniques for details.

By carrying out this process of 'breath-observation-regulation' continuously for long periods of time, the mind not only gets quietened but also sharpened, thereby increasing its concentration power. It thus becomes capable of observing subtler truths about the 'body-mind-intellect complex'. Again, different meditative traditions suggest differing ways of employing this quietened-sharpened mind for the ultimate purpose of experiencing the Reality which transcends the B-M-I complex. The common thread behind all these is to develop the fullest and the sharpest possible awareness of the impermanent nature of all phenomena: "Transient are all the elements of being. Each moment of what we think of as 'our' existence, 'our' life, is a swirl of instantaneous events, continually arising and passing away, it is a well known fact that millions of the cells that make up the living tissue of our bodies are destroyed everyday, and are replaced by new, equally transient ones, so that at every instant there are literally millions of 'deaths' and 'births' occurring in our bodies...This is at the physical level. But at the mental level too, how many more or less clearly formulated thoughts flash through our minds every moment? How many times a day do our intentions, expectations and states of mind fluctuate and change, not infrequently with staggering rapidity?"(8)

As the meditator continuously experiences this Truth of Impermanence through careful observation of unceasingly changing bodily sensations and mental responses to these sensations without identifying 'himself' with these, gradually the accumulated sanskaras get sublimated, and the mind becomes increasingly purified. When this Truth of Impermanence is fully imbibed a complete reorganization of the psyche takes place, for such a person can now function with an exceptional sense of detachment, psychological balance, openness and availability to others. This transmutation, which produces new indelible traits of consciousness, is what is traditionally called 'Enlightenment' or Liberation or Self- realisation(9).

Lord Buddha advocated the aforementioned meditation for development of Insight into impermanence of B-M.I phenomena as the prime method for liberation. Patanjali, and most of other vedantic teachers stress on the other side of the Truth viz. constant recognition of the knower of this ephemeral B-M-I phenomena, the silent unattached Witness within. The meditator is advised to constantly interpret his experiences thus: "You are entirely separate and apart from all desire and thought. You are consciousness, a being deeper than, and fully beyond mind and all its countless modes.— You are not even this 'I' thought which is dearest to you, and to which you are clinging. The true 'I' (the real You within) is a supramental factor. You are pure consciousness and your true identity is 'Conscious Being'. You are the 'thinker' of even the 'I' thought"...[10]. Clearly, an insight into the true nature of 'I' is only complementary to the insight into the Impermance and its full development produces the same result of Enlightenment or Liberation.

Concluding Remarks

The manner in which the four main techniques of inner development have been described above, these may appear to be quite different from each other. This, however, is not the case, for every individual is an integral 'whole' with a mix of faculties of intellect, emotion, action and mentation; the difference being only in the proportion in which these faculties are manifest in different persons. Thus, a person with predominantly intellectual temperament is likely to adopt the Jnana Yoga as his main method, but certainly in order to proceed smoothly on his spiritual journey he cannot but channelise his emotions, actions and thoughts in such a manner as will help in his quest. Thus a knowledge of basic principles (and practice) of the other Yogas is also essential. Similarly, a person bubbling with dynamism (*rajasic temperament*) and activity is best advised to begin his quest from Karma Yoga–the Path of selfless service, but even to do this properly he needs to be aware of the transient nature of sensory pleasures and have some measure of control and purity of mind.

These methods are thus equivalent in more than the usual mathematical sense. The fruition of journey on any one of these paths demands reasonable dexterity in the others too! There is, however, one subtle difference. Since the ultimate purpose of inner development is to transcend the B-M-I complex, ultimately the first three methods, viz. Karma Yoga

Jnana Yoga and Bhakti Yoga will have to be consummated in the Raja Yoga—the Yoga of Meditation, for only through assiduous practice of Meditation can one finally transcend the B-M-I illusion.

NOTES

1. Swami Vivekananda: The Complete Works, Vol. I., Advaita Ashram, Calcutta, 1970 p. 124
2. Swami Vivekananda: The Complete Works, Vol. II., Advaita Ashram, Calcutta, 1970, p. 31
3. Ramana Maharishi: Self-Enquiry (translated by Dr. T.M.P Mahadevan), Sri Ramana- sramam, Tiruvannamalai, 1981.
4. Swami Chinmayananda: Commentary on 'The Holy Geeta', CCMT, Bombay, 1972, Verse II/47.
5. Swami Chidananda: The Path Beyond Sorrow, Divine Life Society, (Tehri Garhwal, UP), 1978, p. 165

   This book, which is a compilation of the sixteen lectures given by swami Chidananda in USA, presents in simple and lucid language the sublime philosophy of Vedanta as applied to our daily life.
6. Patanjali: Patanjal Yoga Darshan, Gita Press, Gorakhpur, 1978, p 83.
7. Amadeo Sole-Leris: Tranquility and Insight, Shambhala, 1986, p. 45
8. ibid, p. 82.
9. ibid, p. 26.
10. Swami Chidananda, opcit, p. 166-167.

8 HOLISTIC VISION OF DEVELOPMENT

"My idea of village Swaraj is that it is a complete republic, independent of its neighbours for its own vital wants, and yet interdependent for many others in which dependence is necessity.... In this structure composed of innumerable villages, there will be ever widening, never ascending circles. Life will not be a pyramid with the apex sustained by the bottom. But it will be an oceanic circle whose centre will be the individual always ready to perish for the village, the latter ready to perish for the circle of villages, till at last the whole becomes one life composed of individuals, never aggressive in their arrogance but ever humble, sharing the majesty of the oceanic circle of which they are integral units. Therefore the outermost circumference will not wield power to crush the inner circle but will give strength to all within and derive its own strength from it. No one will be the first and none the last".

Mahatama Gandhi

We have seen at length in Book I, how the materialistic vision of development, so tenaciously embraced by mankind today is fostering serious maladies threatening the very survival of humanity on this spaceship Earth. Consequently, there is an urgent need to evolve an alternate vision which can ameliorate our present problems and serve as a beacon light to guide us to a peaceful, sustainable and harmonious development. The emerging holistic world view whose gradual evolution has been traced in Book II can clearly form the basis of such an alternative. In this chapter, we shall first discuss the implication of this world view so as to evolve a holistic vision of development. The strategies needed to ensure a smooth transition from our present state to this projected Utopian holistic society will then be discussed at some length.

The Holistic Society

We use the term 'holistic society' to indicate an ideal society, each member of which imbibes-or, at least, is striving to imbibe–the holistic world view. Some important characteristics of such a society can be identified on the basis of our discussions of holistic world view in Chapters 5 and 6. Thus, the recognition that universe is an indivisible whole would automatically lead to harmonious symbiotic coexistence not only within human society but also between human beings and all other living beings viz., trees, birds, animals, insects. etc. Cooperation, rather than competition, would be the parameter governing such a society since all its members would have a nonconflicting common goal, viz., 'self-realisation'-freedom from all sufferings. Such a goal clearly does not give preponderant consideration to achieving things, but it also does not neglect satisfaction of basic physiological needs of the society. In fact such a society will strive to evolve technologies which enable fulfilment of these basic needs (of food, clothing and shelter) for all the people and for all times with minimum effort and in harmony with the higher needs of self realisation, so that people have enough time, energy and inclination to joyously pursue their main goal. The education system, the health care system, the political system etc. will all need to be evolved in such a way that they are conducive to this goal of the society. And obviously in such a holistic society population control will not be difficult since the root causes propelling people to have large families-viz., the old age insecurity and the feeling of 'mine' and 'thine'-are eliminated. An outline of the shape these systems are likely to take is presented below.

Holistic technology

Recalling the main short-comings of the modern industrial technology (which is based on materialistic world view) and the strong influence of world view on technology discussed in Chapter 2, we can easily identify the characteristics of holistic technology. Thus, following the Maslovian model of hierarchy of human needs, we can say that the holistic technology would not only permit satisfaction of all material needs (which is the normally accepted domain of technology), but also not hinder the satisfaction of various higher needs, viz. social, moral and self-actualisation needs(1). Of course, even in satisfaction of material needs, holistic view requires that these needs be satisfied in such a manner that does not threaten their satisfaction in future. It thus immediately follows that:

(a) The holistic technology should not be dependent on exhaustible resources (e.g. fossil fuels, mineral resources of earth, etc.) and should use, as far as possible, only renewable resources of energy as well as matter (e.g. solar energy, biomass, products of photosynthesis etc.) which are freely available to all,

(b) the holistic technology should not create environmental pollution of any kind; for land, air and water are as important physiological needs as food, clothing and shelter,

(c) the holistic technology should be safe at all stages, viz., production, utilisation and ultimate disposal of its waste products.

All these characteristics clearly suggest that in holistic technology, attempt should be to make the fullest use of ecologically sound systems existing in the nature like trees and animals.

Considering the requirement of non-hinderence in the satisfaction of the higher needs it follows that[1],

(d) The holistic technology should promote a sense of social responsibility and cooperation (rather than alienation and privatisation promoted by modern industrial technology), among the producers and users, the ideal clearly being that the users are the producers themselves.

When the users themselves produce for their needs, the waste of precious resources would automatically be curtailed, and as pointed out years ago by Gandhi[2], "the temptation to speed up production indefinitely and at any price disappears. All the endless difficulties and problems that our present-day economic system presents, too, would then come to an end".

Clearly if the users have to produce for their needs, it is also necessary that:

(e) the holistic technology should use only local resources (material as well as human) as far as possible,

(f) In the holistic technology the worker should be "creatively and usefully engaged with both his hands and his brain"[3] so that he can derive that feeling of achievement and satisfaction from work which helps in promoting manifestation of the higher need of self-actualisation.

If we evaluate the modern industrial technology in the light of above mentioned characteristics of holistic technology, it again becomes quite evident that it is a poor agent for promoting integral human welfare, and there is an urgent need to develop alternative technologies. Lest it should seem to be too tall an expectation, some examples of existing holistic technologies may be mentioned here. Fukuoka's[4] natural farming is probably the most outstanding example since it was conceived by Fukuoka only to verify his spiritual experience of omnipotence of Nature and 'meaninglessness' of ego-prompted human interventions in its workings. The result: for over forty years he has demonstrated that the yields obtained by his natural farming are in no way inferior to those obtained by 'modern' industrial farming with the additional benefit that it is environmentally sustainable unlike the modern methods of farming. Gandhi's concept of small scale village and cottage industries[2] is also based on such a holistic view and it needs to be translated into appropriate hardware. The attempts being done at various places to develop gadgets to improve the utilizability of animals are also motivated by the view that draught animal power (in association with biogas plants) has most of the abovementioned characteristics of a holistic technology. Development of mud brick technology to promote low cost holistic housing, improved handloom designs of high productivity, etc. are some other notable attempts in this direction.

It may probably not be out of place to mention here that many of the so-called intermediate technologies being promoted in the rural areas do not fulfil all the requirements of holistic technology enumerated above. Many of them, like photoelectric cells for example, demand production in highly sophisticated factories far away from the place of usage.* Others have been shown to cause pollution (e.g. use of soak pits for waste water disposal has been observed to cause contamination of ground water!). Clearly there is a need to distinguish between simple, small scale technologies and holistic technologies. Though holistic technologies would usually be simple, small scale technologies, the reverse is not true.

An important corollary of the aforementioned characteristics of holistic technology is that a major part of society will have to reorganise itself on the lines of Gandhian village republics, largely selfsufficient in their basic needs[6]. It doesn't of course mean that there should be no heavy industry at all. In fact Gandhi, elaborating his vision of holistic technology had stated in 1940,"...I do visualise electricity, ship buildings, iron works, machine-making and the like existing side by side with village handicrafts. But the order of dependence will be reversed. Hitherto the industrialisation has

---

* Photoelectric cells are in fact suspected to be net energy losers-since a typical cell requires much more energy to build than that collected by it during its entire life span! See Ref. (5).

been so planned as to destroy the villages and village crafts. In the state of the future, it will subserve the villages and their crafts"[6].

Decentralisation of technology goes hand in hand with decentralisation of society, and the mega-metropolis of today can have no place in them. Certainly, Gandhi's prophecy "large cities were a snare and a useless encumbrance and that people would not be happy in them...there would be gangs of thieves and robbers, prostitution and vice flourishing in them and that poor men would be robbed by rich men...."[6] has come true in such metropolitan cities and a holistic society should largely '... consist of groups settled in villages in which voluntary cooperation is the condition of dignified and peaceful existence'[6] Only such a society can be sustained by holistic technology, and only such a society would willingly accept it.

Holistic Education

In Chapter 4 we discussed briefly the degeneration in the modern educational system due to the onslaught of materialistic paradigm. The result: the sole objective of education today remains to secure a good job with a fat salary, and (wherever possible) heavy 'perks'. The pristine concept of education for freedom and enlightenment[7],[8]* seems to have been totally lost, or at best confined to the emblems of educational institutions[9]! Clearly, in the holistic education, the emphasis has to be laid on the inculcation of 'wisdom'-the understanding which liberates Man from perpetual suffering. This doesn't, of course, mean that we ignore the secular education altogether. The ideal of holistic education is beautifully expounded in Isa Upanisad[10], (Verses 9 & 11):

Andham tamah pravisanti ye a vidyam upasate;**

Tato bhuya va te tamo ya uavidyayam ratah

---

* विद्यया अमृतम् अश्नुते

** अन्धंतमः प्रविश्यन्ति ये अविद्याम् उपासते।
ततो भूय इवते तमो य उ विद्यायांरताः।।

"They enter into blinding darkness who worship avidya (secular knowledge) alone; into still greater darkness, as it were, do they enter who delight in vidya (spiritual knowledge) alone"

Vidyam cavidyam ca yastad vedobhayam saha;*

Avidyaya mrtyum tirtva vidyaya amrtamasnute

"He who knows both vidya and avidya together, keeps death at bay through avidya and experiences immortality by means of vidya".

Holistic education thus involves a harmonious blending of the knowledge of the outer world (avidya) and that of the inner-world (vidya). The former**, as it were, enables a man to keep his body and soul together and the later, i.e. 'vidya', the wisdom, leads him to immortality, freedom from all sufferings of the world of change. Today, our educational system deals almost exclusively with 'avidya', and the consequences are before us. There is clearly an urgent need to incorporate in our educational system both theoretical and practical training in inculcating wisdom, as discussed in Chapter 6 and 7. Holistic education will thus have to restore the pristine objective of education, viz., inner development, and the study of physical sciences will be subservient to this objective.

Another important shortcoming of modern education system which has been often pointed out is that it lays preponderant emphasis on 'information transmission' so that neither the curiosity nor the imagination and creativity are stimulated[11-12]. Even the practicals associated with most of the science (and even engineering) courses are stereotyped, predesigned laboratory experiments. Their conclusions are often already known to the students and all that they are

*** विद्याम् च अविद्याम् च यस्तद् वेदउभयं सह।
अविद्याया मृत्युं तीर्त्वा विद्यया अमृतमश्नुते।।

**Viz., the knowledge of the outer world, i.e. the Science

expected to do is to fill in the blanks of the handouts with experimental observations and perform some calculations using the formulae already listed in the handout.

The result: the educational process becomes drab and didactic—a veritable burden which the students wish to shed off at the earliest. Clearly, there is a need to make the process of acquiring knowledge as enjoyable as playing. Some successful attempts in this direction have already been made[13].

The main distinguishing features of this free progress education for children should be to allow students to choose their pace of learning; minimizing the lecturing by teachers and motivating students to acquire knowledge on their own through use of library facilities, experimentation, observation of environment, visits to museums, science parks etc., with teachers acting only as guides, promoting cooperation through group activities and eliminating (cut-throat) competition by removal of formal tests and examinations[13].

Another important feature of the holistic educational system should be to emphasize on developing problem solving abilities rather than on memorizing the information available in books. In this context, creativity and intuition are probably the most important, and yet these have been ignored in the modern educational system. Recent researches have conclusively demonstrated that these abilities can also be 'developed' like other abilities (e.g., arithmatical skills) and special courses and training programmes developed for this purpose are becoming increasingly popular[14]. These should naturally occupy a special place in the holistic education, for creativity is one of our important higher needs. Only young men and women with creative minds and innovative thinking can be expected to develop new holistic technologies and willingly accept the holistic way of living.

Holistic Health Care

The term for 'healthy' in Sanskrit is Swastha which literally means 'anchored in the self'. This indicates that real health encompasses 'total well being', movement towards one's identity with the realself and not merely absence of physical pain or a handsome body structure.

Keeping this in mind, the holistic health care should not merely restrict itself to symptomatic pain suppression but rather incorporate the physiological, psychological and spiritual dimensions in its approach. Moreover, the close interconnectedness of body, mind and the environment is to be duly appreciated in diagnosing as well as treatment of an ailment. We have already seen in Chapter 5 how the recognition of short-comings of modern medicine is forcing the people to try alternative systems of medicine like Homoeopathy, Naturopathy, Ayurveda, Unani, Tibetan systems, etc. Also, holistic techniques like Yoga, biofeedback and meditation are also being progressively used particularly for various psychosomatic diseases. In the light of available experiences, we can easily visualise a judicious integration of these systems of health care in a holistic health centre.

As in the modern hospitals, the patients in these centres would have twin accesses, viz. one through emergency services and the other through regular out-patient's department. It seems that for emergency situations needing immediate relief e.g., accidents with heavy loss of blood and injuries needing surgical intervention, strokes (like asthama attacks, cereberal haemhorrage, paralysis etc.), poisoning, snake bites, heart attacks etc.—allopathic medicines are the best available option. After a certain degree of stability of the patient's condition, he could then be treated on the OPD pattern suggested below to reduce the likely side-effects of 'strong' allopathic medicines.

In the OPD of a holistic health centre, the patients would be first examined by a physician expert in diagnosing diseases by examination of the pulse. Such physicians are still available in Ayurvedic, Unani and Tibetan schools of medicine. It may be pointed out that the art and science of diagnosis by just feeling the pulse (which has got completely neglected in the face of sophisticated medical instrumentation) has a lot of merit and should find an important place in holistic health care. Based on this diagnosis and the acknowledged efficiency of various systems of medicine in treating different diseases, the patient would be directed to an appropriate physician or surgeon. Thus, for treating chronic skin ailments like eczema, warts etc.; chronic respiratory troubles like Asthama; chronic bone diseases like spondylysis, arthritis etc.; eye troubles like cataract, homoeopathy could be the first choice. For digestive disorders, hypertension, cardiac deficiencies and general debility ayurveda could be the first choice; for psychological problems, Yoga and meditation could be the first choice; for clearly identified bacterial illness like malaria allopathy could be the first choice, and for most of acute diseases like mild fevers, bad cold, headache, indigestion etc., fasting and nature cure could be the first choice, and so on. These areas of special efficiency indicated here are clearly based on authors' subjective experiences and could be better decided after a free and frank dialogue between experts of these various systems of medicine. Such a dialogue would certainly be feasible in a holistic society where the physicians' objective would be to cure their patients completely and at the earliest rather than maximizing their earnings (or using them as guinea pigs for research), as in our modern society. Besides prescribing medicines for the specific diseases, the physicians of holistic health centre would also advise the patient on the type of diet which would be most suitable for him and some physical and mental exercises (i.e. yoga and meditation practices) which would catalyse the process of recovery and thereafter help him maintain good health.

Keeping in view the objective of holistic health care, viz., achieving a state of physical and mental well being, and not just freedom from disease it is quite natural that diet reform, yoga and meditation practices would form the most important constituent of the health centre. The physicians of holistic health centres would therefore have to be fully trained in these practices irrespective of the system of medicine followed by them.

Political and Economic System

In the modern society, the political and economic system is given preponderant importance due to their power and influence in determining the material well-being of the society and especially of the people involved in it. In the holistic society, where material well-being is of secondary importance, these systems too would naturally lose their excessive charm and significance. Business and politics would be like any other profession, motivated only by the concern for welfare of all and not by the desire for amassing wealth and exercising power.

In a holistic society based on the concept of Gandhian 'village republic', the political activity will confine itself to election of a governing body—a Panchayat—which would look after various day-to-day administrative and, as and when necessary, law-and- order problems of the village. Only those persons would be eligible for becoming members of the panchayat who are generally acknowledged to have attained certain degree of proficiency in holistic education. It will be the duty of this panchayat to ensure that the basic minimum needs of all residents of the village are provided in time, that the common property and service facilities of the community, e.g. tubewells for irrigation of fields and drinking water supply, biogas plants and other energy systems, cold storage, health centre, school, village industries centre, community hall, play grounds etc. are well maintained, and to ensure an equitable distribution of net income of the village among the residents. And abcve all, the panchayat will act as a watch-dog to ensure that members of the village keep up their tempo of inner-development and will devise suitable catalysing activities like regular yoga and meditation camps, community celebration of festivals, interaction with self-realised saints, group discussions on matters of interest to the community etc.

In a holistic society, since the emphasis is on self-realisation and not on amassing wealth, private property would naturally be confined to the very basic personal necessities which will all be provided by the community. The economic activity of such a typical village would, therefore, mainly be that of bartering its surplus production with other similar villages in the neighbourhood, and ensuring proper storage and distribution of the essential goods within the community.

Of course, the introduction of village republics does not imply that there would be no nation state, or cities. Cities would also have an important role to play in that these would cater to special requirements like higher education, administration, trade, special health care facilities etc. of a cluster of such villages. But as discussed later, these cities would be much different from modern parasitic cities.

Strategies for Transition

The elaborate discussion of a holistic society of future presented above would become meaningful only if we are able to visualise the steps needed to bring about the transition from the present to the projected utopia. Such a visualisation can be confidently done only by a self-realised person—one who is in complete harmony with the nature and has crossed the barriers of time and space, since he can directly 'see' the consequences of his suggestions. For ordinary mortals like the authors, to prescribe steps for transition of society is clearly too presumptuous a task. And yet we are undertaking it in all humility since it is due to the lack of any concrete suggestions in this regard that the whole concept of holistic world view and holistic society are rejected today as impracticable fantasies of some idealists.

A little reflection reveals that the first and the most urgent step needed in this direction is to create an awareness amongst the masses of the serious problems associated with materialistic paradigm and the need for switchover to a holistic way of living. This clearly needs a massive mass-education compaign, and all the available mass communication media could be used for this purpose. The efficacy of antinuclear compaigns in the west and of 'save the trees' (Chipko) movements in our own country gives a hope that such mass education compaigns are not always fruitless.

Of course, a mere intellectual understanding is not sufficient to bring about the desired change in world view. As discussed at length in Chapter 7, correction in the perception of reality needs a thorough internal reorganisation of our psyche, which can best be done through meditative practices like Vipassana. Therefore, alongwith a mass-education compaign, there is a need for motivating people to take to these non-sectarian, universally acceptable meditative practices which are free from shackles of any organised religion. The motivation could come in a variety of forms, e.g., in our own country, Rajasthan state Government grants leave on full pay to the teachers of schools for participation in 10-day Vipassana meditation camps. This could easily be extended to all employees in the organised sector- public or private. Introduction of such mental training in the schools and colleges—on the pattern of compulsory physical training—would also be necessary to catalyse the process of transition to a holistic society.

All the above enumerated measures of inner-transformation are, due to the very nature of the task involved, likely to show perceptible results only after a long time and that too only if these are very enthusiastically propagated. The process of inner development is a very arduous one, and is most efficient when conducted at a modest pace, especially in its initial phases when a person has to exert a lot in swimming against the tide of materialistic world view. This process can however be accelerated and made less strenuous if simultaneously the systemic transformations indicated below are initiated.

The most important, and certainly the most challenging transformation needed to accelerate the acceptance of the holistic world view is to initiate the process of de-urbanisation— i.e. a gradual, systematic dismantling of the megametropolis in consonance with our visualisation of the holistic society based on self-sufficient village republics. It is obvious that a sudden dismemberment of big cities into smaller 'village republics' is not practically feasible since these parasitic cities are dependent on surrounding (and sometime even far off) villages even for their basic essential needs, and the land available for cultivation in cities is too little to suffice for their enormous population. A strategy to bring about this transition smoothly will therefore necessarily involve a number of phases. The first phase, which could, in fact, be immediately implemented, is to halt all new building construction work in the cities, and instead promote setting up of self-sufficient communes of 100-200 families each far away from the cities. Preliminary calculations for Indian conditions show[15] that such a typical commune for

100 families should be able to meet all its basic material needs using available holistic technologies (viz. organic farming with animal power, biogas/biomass for fuel and other energy needs like electricity for illumination, irrigation and water pumping etc.) and generate enough surplus (e.g. of milk, sugar, vegetables etc.) if it is provided with about 50 hectares of cultivable land and 200 cattle, by no means an infeasible proposition even if we consider the presently cultivated land and the present cattle population of the country[16]. The establishment of even one such commune each, in the proximity of major cities would give a tremendous fillip to the process of transformation for it will act as a live demonstration of the benefits of holistic society. And as even a few of these communes demonstrate their viability and the potential for convivial living—free from hustle and bustle, stresses and strains of modern urban life—surely many more of such communes would spring up automatically. In fact these communes could be viewed as holistic alternatives to the cooperative housing societies mushrooming today in all cities, and should be encouraged by the government through financial support and other incentives.* With all new construction stopped, and migration of city dwellers to such communes increasing steadily, it should be possible to reduce the population level of most of the cities within 30-40 years to such an extent that a majority of the remaining inhabitants of the cities can also form communes within the boundaries of the erstwhile city to complete the process of transition. In our visualisation of the holistic society the cities will also have an important role to play. Besides being the centre of federal government and defence forces, the city will lookafter facilities for communications, inter-commune trade and storage of surpluses, specialised medical care, higher education, appellant court, specialised industries etc.

---

*In Canada, the federal Department of Environment funded the Ark Project designed by the New Alchemy Institute to demonstrate the feasibility of a small-scale sustained-yield food production in a closed ecological circuit[19].

The personnel engaged in these jobs could be easily supported using a fraction of the surplus generated by the communes, which could be viewed as a tax paid by the communes to the federal 'government' for providing these facilities. In addition, the rural development activity should also be promoted on these lines thus transforming present villages into such self-sufficient communes.

Development of holistic technologies would be a natural long-term outcome of the evolution of such self-sufficient communes. However, the process could be greatly accelerated if suitable changes are made in the curricula of the various professional institutes (especially, medical and engineering colleges) in accordance with the requirements of holistic education discussed above, so that the engineers and doctors who come out of these institutes are motivated and trained to think and work in this direction. Such changes can however be made and implemented only if we have sufficient number of trained teachers who have themselves imbibed—or at least, are sincerely striving to imbibe—the holistic world view. Therefore a massive teacher's training programme should be launched with the help of upcoming organisations like VIA (Vipassana International Academy, Igatpuri) devoted exclusively to this task so that within next 5- 7 years the teachers thus trained could impart holistic education both in schools and colleges. Meanwhile, a modest beginning in this direction could be immediately made with the help of teachers already convinced of this need and striving for inner development on their own.

The holistic health care centres envisaged above could probably be set up immediately and would receive full support and patronage from all sections of the society groaning under the ill-effects of modern medicine. In fact, a few such centres have already sprung up in the west and have been influential in changing the life styles and dietary habits of their patrons. In order to replicate such centres in large numbers it is necessary that an integrated system of medicine and health care be carefully evolved after an extensive debate between the practitioners of various systems of medicine. The government health department and even WHO could initiate such discussions through seminars/workshops and promote setting up of holistic health care centres based on their recommendations. Needless to add, the success of such centres would also contribute towards acceptance of the holistic world view and the holistic way of living.

Epilogue

A mere visualisation of the holistic society of the future, and of the strategies needed to bring about this change—even if it is correct, is not sufficient to actually transform the society. The question which remains unanswered till now is: who is actually going to implement these policy changes? Clearly, if political leaders could be convinced of the need for this transformation, the rest would automatically follow. The onus for bringing about this transformation thus indirectly shifts again to those intellectuals who are already convinced of this need, for it is they who can, by example and precept, convince others of the gravity of the situation and the need for change. In view of the alarming rate of increase of the serious problems facing the society today, it is evident that the time available for action is rather limited. If you, the reader, are now convinced that such a transformation is essential for the survival of humanity, why not do something to help this process, for as Jesus taught: who ever knows what is right to do and fails to do it, for him it is a sin!

NOTES

1. Dhar, P.L., *'Holistic technology—A Conceptual Framework'*, Gandhi Marg, 108, March 1988, p. 755-763.
2. Gandhi, M.K., *"Village Industries"*, Navjivan Publishing House, Ahmedabad, 1960, p. 13.
3. Schumacher, E.F., *Small is Beautiful*, Abacus, 1974, pp. 24.
4. Fukuoka, M., *The one-straw Revolution: An Introduction to Natural Farming*, published in India by Friends Rural Centre, Rasulia, 1984.
5. Odum, H.T. and E.C. Odum: *Energy basis for Man and Nature*, McGraw Hill, NY, 1976, p. 179.
6. Dhar, P.L.: *Gandhian Vision of Technology*, Gandhi Marg, Vol. 18, Jan. 1989, p. 648-656.
7. Isa Upanisad, verse 11.
8. 'Education is the manifestation of perfection already in Man.... The end of all education, all training, should be man-making' from *Swami Vivekananda's writing on Education*, compiled by T S Avinashilingam, R K Mission Vidyalya, Coimbatore.
9. Thus, the cryptic phrase 'Vidyaya amrtam asnute' is inscribed in the emblem of National Council of Educational Research and Training but its import is yet to be reflected in the text-books developed by NCERT.
10. Swami Ranganathananda, *'The Message of Upanisads'*, Bhartiya Vidya Bhavan, 1987, p. 134.
11. Risi, M.: Macroscole-*A holistic approach to Science Teaching*, Discussion paper, Science Council of Canada, 1982.
12. Illich, Ivan: De Schooling Society, Penguin.
13. Personal Discussions with Director of Mirambika, a free progress unit of Sri Aurbindo Educational Society, New Delhi.
14. Khandwala, P.N., *'Fourth Eye-Excellence through Creativity'*, A.H. Wheeler and Co., Allahabad, 1984.
15. Rawat, V.S. and Vinod Fonia: *Alternate Technology Models for Integral human welfare*, B. Tech. project report, Mech. Engg. Deptt., IIT Delhi, 1984.
16. Considering that the agricultural lands cultivated in 1976 in India amounted to 143 m hectares [17], it is 'technically feasible' to support upto 1400 m people in such communes. Of course, the cattle population (at present about 80 m) will have to be increased

multifold even to support our present population. This could be easily achieved during the transition period of 30-40 years, by cutting down on animal slaughter for meat etc.

Considering the fact that the population density elsewhere in the world is much smaller, it should be feasible to support the population of the globe on a small fraction of the presently available agricultural land of about 1.43 billion hectares[(18)].

17. *The State of India's Environment*, 1982, A Citizen's Report, Centre for Science & Environments, New Delhi, p. 3.

18. Myers, N. (Ed.): *The GAIA Atlas of Planet Management*, Pan Books, London, 1985, p. 24.

19. *Canada as a Conserver Society*, Report No. 27, Science Council of Canada, 1977, p. 94.